Balbi. *Essai statistique...*

ESSAI STATISTIQUE

SUR

LES BIBLIOTHÈQUES

DE VIENNE

PRÉCÉDÉ

DE LA STATISTIQUE DE LA

BIBLIOTHÈQUE IMPÉRIALE

COMPARÉE

aux plus grands établissemens de ce genre anciens et modernes
et suivi d'un

APPENDICE

offrant la statistique des Archives de Venise et de la collection technologique
formée par S. M. l'Empereur Ferdinand I., un coup d'oeil sur les progrès de
la civilisation, de l'industrie, du commerce et de la population dans la Monarchie
Autrichienne, terminé par le tableau statistique de ses grandes divisions
administratives rédigé d'après les derniers recensemens.

Par Adrien Balbi.

A VIENNE,

CHEZ FRÉDÉRIC VOLKE.

1835.

Adriano Balbi

A Statistical Essay on the Libraries of Vienna and the World

Translated by
Larry Barr and Janet L. Barr

McFarland & Company, Inc., Publishers
Jefferson, North Carolina, and London

Translation of original 1835 title (see frontispiece)

Statistical Essay
on
the Libraries
of Vienna
preceded
by the statistics of the
Imperial Library
compared
to the largest establishments of that type ancient and modern
and followed by an
appendix
providing the statistics of the Venetian archives and the technical
collection formed by His Majesty Emperor Ferdinand I, a glance at the
progress of civilization, industry, commerce and population in the
Austrian Monarchy, [and] ending with a statistical table of the major
administrative divisions written after the last census.
by Adriano Balbi
at Vienna.
Frédéric Volke
1835

Library of Congress Cataloguing-in-Publication Data

Balbi, Adriano, 1782–1848.
  Statistical essay on the libraries of Vienna and the world.

  Translation of: Essai statististique sur les bibliothèques
de Vienne
  1. Österreichische Nationalbibliothek.
2. Libraries — History. 3. Library statistics.
4. Libraries — Austria — Vienna — History. 5. Libraries —
Austria — Vienna — Statistics. I. Barr, Larry, 1938– ,
cotranslator. II. Barr, Janet L., 1941– , cotranslator.
III. Title.
Z794.O86B3413   1986   027.0436′13   84-43235

ISBN 0-89950-149-4   (acid-free natural paper)

Printed in the United States of America.

McFarland   Box 611   Jefferson NC 28640

Table of Contents

Translators' Preface

Among the innumerable debates raging among European scholars in the early nineteenth century, one of the minor ones was concerned with library statistics. An important participant in that scholarly melee was Adriano Balbi, whose first name appears on most of the title pages of his several works in the French style, Adrien. In this translation of his 1835 essay on libraries from a statistical point of view – libraries worldwide, not merely Viennese as his title indicates – the reader will encounter the names of other scholars who participated in this debate before 1835. A brief bibliography of them was provided by Balbi (see pages 49–50).

An important aspect of the debate to be found in these pages concerns the divergences reported for library holdings at about the same period of time by different writers. For example one writer reported 400,000 volumes in the Royal Library in Paris in 1819; four years later another author reported 800,000 volumes for the same library. These kinds of enormous differences commonly occur in the various statistical comparisons that were published early in the last century, and as the reader will see, Balbi was concerned about this. Indeed he was concerned with the question of what utility all these numbers might have, and that is a question that continues to concern librarians. Almost a century and a half has passed since Balbi's essay was first published in which he expressed the view that even if one knew exactly how many volumes, manuscripts, coins, etc., every library had that still would not indicate how important or useful the collection was. Usefulness and importance lie rather in what kind of books are available, how important each book is – in short, he argued, 1,000 volumes of a certain kind in a certain place might be of more value than 20,000 or 30,000 of another kind or in another place. In making this sort of argument he anticipated the concern of modern librarians for measures of library effectiveness.*

*Balbi was involved, as well, in the larger debate from which the science of statistics was to emerge. Before 1850 or so, statistics largely related to counting things, usually

ix

Of course, most of the librarians now practicing their art never heard of Balbi but the translators think he deserves a new audience even if it is limited to only a few scholars. There is no thorough biography of the man in English, but in his own time he was well-known. He was born in Venice in 1782 and died in his native province in 1848. Most of his contemporaries would have considered him a geographer rather than a statistician, and that is still an appropriate way to consider his life and career. His most enduring work was *Abrégé de Géographie*, first published in 1832, which went through many editions and was translated into several languages. 1832 is also the year Balbi went to Vienna as a counselor for statistics and geography to the Imperial Court. Thus an Italian* scholar produced one of the first attempts at systematizing library statistics using French, the international language of his time, as part of his work for the monarchy in Vienna, a German-speaking city. And Balbi's command of French was not exemplary. His sentence construction and choice of words was often torturous. Dr. Charles Janssens, whose expertise was of great help to the translators, notes that Balbi overused superlatives, was windy, used punctuation practically at random, played around with his pronouns, and used an extremely involved style. His observations are quite correct. What Balbi had to say is often very interesting, but he simply was not able to write in a readable style.

Translators have some duty to preserve an author's style as well as to convey his meaning and that is what has been attempted here. The result, unfortunately, is not English prose of the highest quality. Referring to Janssens again, in a letter to the translators, he says that the main characteristic of the book is "the extremely complex nature of the French text" which does not lend itself "to a good English translation. Indeed, it is strictly a text with a large number of tangential clauses, subordinated to one another, which, standing alone, mean

(cont.) producing numerical data relating to government. One gets some insight into the scholarly struggle in his fiery defense of his Abrégé *against its critics and those who had dared to use or even alter his data without authorization. (See Appendix 7.) The second half of this volume is devoted not to libraries but to Balbi's interests in the larger fields of geography and statistics. Some of the methods he employs seem very crude now, perhaps of interest only to those savants who study the history of statistical methods and their applications, but they are a reflection of a lively intellect that had an impact in the early nineteenth century.*

*Venetia and most of the old Venetian Republic as it had existed before the Napoleonic Wars was annexed to Austria in 1814–15. Technically, therefore, Balbi was a Venetian but was in his later life a citizen of the Austrian Empire. Sketches of his life appear in several national biography sets. For examples see the following: Biographisches Lexikon des Kaiserthums Österreich, *Wien, 1856, vol. 1; and* Nouvelle Biographie Générale..., *Paris, 1855, vol. 4; and* Enciclopedia Italiani di Scienze, Lettere ed Arti, *1930–38, vol. 5.*

nothing; if included in the sentences, the unwieldiness becomes such that the original thought or main idea is drowned out and practically forgotten, making the reading of such a text extremely laborious." Perhaps this is why Balbi has been overlooked by twentieth century librarians.

He was not, however, ignored by librarians in the nineteenth century. For example, Reuben Aldridge Guild, the librarian at Brown University, in what is often considered the first American textbook on library science, referred to Balbi as being "next to the elaborate Article by Ebert, ...the first statistical View of existing Libraries to be at all relied upon for general Accuracy..."* Also, he was quoted at some length in the 1876 Report,† a few pages being translated into English, but mostly reproducing statistical tables. The translated pages were obviously considered the best available explication of the problems involved in comparing library statistics. It is clear, then, that for several decades after his death Balbi's approach to the problems of library statistics was considered worthwhile, perhaps even seminal. His contribution deserves to be remembered.

And now, a personal word: Dr. Charles L. Janssens, a wonderful friend and an extraordinary linguist, has made many invaluable suggestions for this work that have made it a great deal more readable than it otherwise would have been. A native of Belgium, French is his mother tongue, but he is fluent in several languages — Greek, Latin, Dutch, Spanish, Italian, German, Farsi, and, of course, English. We first became acquainted in Ahwaz, Iran, in 1977, shortly before the revolution. He was then the dean of the College of Foreign Languages and Literatures at Jundi Shapur University. We were there to establish a library school. Even then his marvelous language skills often came to our aid. It is a great pleasure to acknowledge both his warm friendship and his scholarly aid.

> Larry & Janet Barr
> Boone, North Carolina
> Summer, 1985

Guild, Reuben A. The Librarian's Manual. *New York: Charles B. Norton, 1858. Reprinted by Grand River Books, Detroit, 1971. page 46.*
†*U.S. Bureau of Education.* Public Libraries in the United States of America: Their History, Condition, and Management; Special Report, Part I. *Washington, D.C.: Government Printing Office, 1876. Reprinted by University of Illinois, Graduate School of Library Science, n. d., pages 745–758.*

Introduction

Vienna, like all the great capitals of Europe, has been described with all possible details in a host of works and by a large number of travelers. This one, enchanted by its picturesque location, in the middle of a vast, fertile plain of varying aspect and watered by one of the greatest rivers of Europe, took greater pleasure in describing the beauty of its immediate surroundings, the hills adorned with beautiful vineyards, the luxuriant meadows where large herds graze, the pretty and flourishing villages, the elegant country estates which crown their summits and the snow-covered peaks, which, toward the south, delineate its vast horizon. That one, as he was contemplating the rustic islets formed by the several arms of the majestic Danube, so rich in reminders of all the eras, from the fabulous myths and the historic times of Greece and Rome to the bloody incursions of the Barbarians, to the terrible attacks of the Ottomans and to the memorable battles waged in our own days, took it to heart to focus on all the places that played an important role in the long succession of centuries. Another yet, struck by the exquisite beauty of Vienna's promenades, takes pleasure in describing the magnificent view one enjoys touring its boulevards, from where one overlooks the immense grass-covered meadow, which separates the city from the suburbs, and whose long symmetrical lines, flanked by trees [and] formed by the main roads and by-ways which run through it in all directions, lit by night by several thousands of lamps, create the effect of a superb illumination. Then he describes the attractive garden of the *Belvedere* and the *Augarten*, once the favorite residence of Joseph II and gathering spot of the high society but for several years now almost entirely deserted; finally, the *Prater*, a vast forest, located at the gates of Vienna, which he claims to be the most lovely of all European promenades because of its lush vegetation, its numerous cafes, restaurants and popular amusement places which dot it, and the very large numbers of elegant strollers who visit it every day on foot, on horseback and in magnificent carriages.

Other writers seem to have assigned themselves the task of

1

describing the superb *Cathedral of St. Etienne*, with its memories reaching far back in time, its bold spire, which a lively writer, M. Marmier, finds more imposing than the one of Strasburg, more elegant than the one of Ulm, more majestic than the one of Antwerp; the *Burg-Thor*, magnificent propylaeum, which, from afar, announces to the traveler the entrance of the Caesars' residence, the work of the celebrated Nobile, who, with a remarkable talent, succeeded in combining simplicity and elegance with the strength that a monument of that kind required; and the *Manège*, that part of the Imperial Palace which was planned by the genius of *Fischer of Erlach*, justly renowned for its architecture, for its colossal dimensions and for the brilliant feasts given there by the Court as well as the concerts, which eight to nine hundred musicians executed with admirable harmony.

The masterpieces of sculpture which embellish some churches and some public monuments, the magnificent painting galleries, the superb collections of prints, the rarities and precious objects preserved in the Imperial Treasure and in the Belvedere, the wealth of plant life offered by the thirty-two botanical gardens of Vienna and of its surrounding areas, which, if they were assembled in one establishment, would perhaps constitute the richest botanical garden in the world; the magnificent greenhouses of *Schönbrunn* and the charming unity of this Imperial Castle, the bizarre curiosities of the vast park of *Laxenburg*, with its Gothic castle, faithful mirror of the customs and traditions of the Middle Ages' most brilliant epoch of chivalry; the delights of the castles and parks of *Dornbach, Pötzleinsdorf*, etc., etc., those of [the castle and park of] *Baden*, so brilliant, so animated during the season of the waters; those of *Weilburg*, magnificent country-seat of His Imperial Highness Archduke Charles, situated in the romantic valley of St. Helène (Helenenthal); all these places, all these objects and a host of others have been described in their most minute details and justly appreciated in more than one work.

Eloquent writers, gifted with great powers of observation, have described the courteous and amiable welcome extended to strangers; the feasts, the popular amusements, the luxury and good taste displayed by prominent people and rich owners in their palaces; the elegant dress and the attractiveness of the beautiful Viennese [women]; their talent for painting and music; their remarkable education; the ease with which they speak all the main languages of Europe and the tactfulness with which they pass judgment over their literatures. Very competent and impartial judges have rated the main artists of the theater of the Court as first rank among the actors of Germany; and a spirited author, making an accurate comparison between the two capitals, of France and of Austria, observes that *Vienna* is to *melodies* what *Paris* is to *fashion*, for these are the two great cities from which both [melodies and fashion respectively] emanate quickly to every country of the globe where European civilization prevails.

Profound philosophers such as M. *Cousin*, lively and eloquent writers such as MM. *Marmier, St. Marc-Girardin, Menzel, Wilibald Alexis*, etc., etc., *Reviews*, edited by conscientious scholars profoundly versed in the subjects they have undertaken to treat, such as the *Revue Britannique*, the *Revue Germanique*, the *France Littéraire* and other French, English and German journals have already brought to light the development displayed by industry in all its branches, the state of literature of the sciences and of the fine arts, and the [growth of] public instruction and of the administration not only in the capital of Austria but also of the whole of the Austrian Monarchy. It is in these works, it is in these periodicals that a large number of facts are recorded,* [facts] as important as generally unknown. But, to our great astonishment, not a single author, not a single journal has as yet brought out the full importance of the numerous libraries, of the rich collections of natural history of antiquities and of technology, which, in this respect, assign such a distinguished rank to that city among the greatest capitals of Europe. It is no surprise therefore that more than one scholar, among those who gathered there during the congress of German naturalists held in Vienna in 1832, should have expressed his astonishment at finding it so richly provided in this type of establishment.

The important facts, of which we had had knowledge in Paris by perusing the *Vaterländische Blätter*, had already revealed a considerable part of these treasures to us. We have recorded the most important ones in the description of the Austrian Empire of the *Abrégé de Géographie*. The knowledge of these same facts had naturally led us to suspect the existence of a much larger number yet as we were observing the august Monarch — who was just lowered into his tomb — cultivate with such perseverance several branches of literature and of the natural sciences, knowing with what ardor all the members of the Imperial Family devoted themselves, each on his own account, to the special study of one or several different sciences, and upon learning that the two ministers, who were at the head of the affairs of the Empire, His Highness, the Prince of Metternich for everything that concerns foreign relations and His Eminence, Count of Kolowrat for everything that concerns domestic matters, were themselves versed in more than one science and possessed libraries as numerous as carefully selected. Such high and noble examples could not remain without

*See Appendix 2, beginning on page 90.

emulators among the great and among the opulent persons of the capital of the Empire.

Our relations with its most distinguished scholars and the researches which we have made on this subject yielded results fully corroborating our conjectures, and we found that a city, whose permanent population exceeds hardly* two-fifths of that of Paris and to which *tourists* have reserved the unjust reproach "that its inhabitants think only of amusing themselves and of stuffing themselves," does not possess less than *45 public* or *private libraries, 15 collections of mineralogy, 20†* of zoology and of *anatomical displays, 23* of *antiquities*, of *instruments of physics*, of *astronomy*, of *technology* and of *heraldry*, and *20* of *medals.* And do not believe that these are shabby collections, composed of a few hundred items; there are several in this number which can stand up to the first of their type which Europe possesses, a fact of which the reader can convince himself by perusing the statistics of the libraries that we offer him, and by reading the two theses that we intend to publish, [one] on the collections of natural history, [the other] on those of antiquities and numismatics. To lend support to what we have just stated, we shall add here solely that the *technological collection*, formed by His Majesty the young king of Hungary, today *Emperor Ferdinard I.*, is the first one to exist and counts not less than 41,500 items§; that the precious *medal displays* of *M. Baron of Bretfeld* and of *M. Aulic Counselor of Welzel* are composed, the first one of more than 30,000 and the second one of about 25,000 items; that the *herbarium* of *M. Dr. Endlicher*, employee of the Imperial Library, does not count less than 20,000 species; that the one of the illustrious botanist *Baron Jacquin* counts close to three-fourths of that number; and that the one of *M. Zahlbruckner*, private secretary of His Imperial Highness Archduke Jean, has 15,000 of them, among which all the species which form the *Flora of the empire of Austria*, and, what is more, the complete *alpine Flora* known *in Europe.*

We were entirely engrossed with the draft of the *Premiers Eléméns de Géographie*, already a long time promised to the public, and of the *Essai d'un Tableau Statistique de la Terre,* ** when the publi-

---

*See Appendix 4, p. 101.

†*In 1823,* 38 collections of mineralogy *and* 37 of zoology and anatomical displays *were counted. The purchase of several series made by the government to complete those of the public establishments, a few sales abroad and others, more numerous, made to scholars of the Empire residing outside of Vienna, of the inevitable dispersions which sometimes follow the demise of the possessors of these collections, explain the noteworthy diminution that we have just pointed out.*

§*See Appendix 5, p. 103.*

**See Appendix 7.*

cation of the *Histoire de la Bibliothèque Impériale* by M. Aulic Counselor de Mosel,* who is its first keeper, gave us the idea of comparing this establishment with the largest ancient and modern libraries. The kindness that the Count of Dietrichstein, who is its prefect, grants us and the endless courtesies that were extended to us, thanks to his protection, by all the employees of the Library, have given us the determination to complete this project. The material, which we had previously collected on the statistics of the main libraries of the two hemispheres, have strongly contributed to abridge the work which we have the honor to offer to the public. We hope that they will receive it with the favorable response they have given our previous works. Despite its slender volume, this work is nonetheless the result of a large number of long and difficult studies, which have resulted not only in filling one of the main gaps presented by this branch of statistics, but also to rectify several errors, admitted already long ago as incontestable truths, and to destroy a few presumptions, which were no less widespread.

We have thought it necessary to bolster by some positive facts — though they may not yet be widely known — the opinions we have voiced either in this preliminary discourse or in the body of the work,† and also to improve this opportunity to raise our just complaints about the publication of the *Hausbuch des geographischen Wissens*§ as well as to announce the one of the *Tableau Statistique de la Terre*, which we intend to publish in the beginning of 1836. All this constitutes the Appendix, which follows the Statistical Essay on the Libraries of Vienna.

We have nothing further to add to this subject, having already cited, as we customarily do, at the respective passages, the numerous sources from which we have drawn, and having already named all the praiseworthy scholars, national and foreign, who have been willing to help us with their advice and their knowledge in the solution of the difficult problem that we have undertaken to solve.

---

*Geschichte der kaiserl. konigl. Hofbibliothek zu Wien, von Fr. Ig. Edlen von Mosel, k.k. wirkl. Hofrathe und erstem Custos der Hofbibliothek. *Vienna 1835. 1 vol. in 8°. This work has already brought to its scholarly author the most flattering distinctions on the part of several sovereigns; the King of Prussia presented him with a golden snuffbox; the King of Saxony with a large golden medal; and Her Majesty Archduchess Marie Louise sent him a ring with her monogram filled with diamonds.*

†*See Appendix 2, p. 90, as well as the facts contained in Appendix 6.*
§*See Appendix 7.*

I. Origin of the Library

Among the great public collections of books presently in existence, there are very few which can boast of a more ancient and more illustrious origin than that of the *Imperial Library*, which adorns the modern capital of the Caesars. According to the Aulic Counselor, M. de Mosel, who has just published its history, the founding of this magnificent establishment goes back to the year 1440, a year forever engraved in the annals of mankind, it being the same one generally agreed upon to commemorate the invention of printing with movable type. It was at that time that Emperor Frederick III. (V.) of the House of Hapsburg, one of the princes of the Middle Ages who most honored letters and scholars, ordered his books and manuscripts arranged in such a way as to form a systematic collection. The renowned scholars who carried out this task were Eneas Sylvius Piccolomini, later to become so famous under the name of Pope Pius II., and Georges Purbach, a very distinguished mathematician, astronomer and man of letters.

Several established facts are witness of what we have just stated about the honorable position that the Imperial Library occupies with respect to the antiquity of its founding. We borrow them from works of Abbots *Andres* and *Morelli*, and from those of MM. *Wilken, Ebert, Wachler, Blume, Jäck, Petit-Radel, Valery* and others whom it would take too long to name. We have arranged them in a table in order to render them more conspicuous and to facilitate comparison. However, these facts must be introduced by some remarks in order to avoid any criticism of inaccuracy which anyone less versed in these matters might formulate against us.

We have excluded from this table a large number of libraries — famous during the Middle Ages — because they no longer exist, or else because of their prolonged status quo their importance wanes when compared to the immense collections which have since been gathered. It is in this category that must be included the *libraries* of a few *cathedrals*, and especially those of several *monasteries*, which during the centuries of ignorance preserved for us the masterpieces of the Greeks and of the Romans, constantly maintained lit in their peaceful retreats the sacred torch of the sciences and the literatures, and were for both hemispheres so many centers from which enlightenment spread in all directions.

Several scholars consider the *Vatican Library* as the oldest of Europe by tracing its beginnings to Pope St. Hilary, who gathered some manuscripts in his palace of St. John of Lateran in 465. But we shall adhere to the more likely opinion set forth by the scholar Ebert, who dates its founding only from the year 1417, at which time it passed from Avignon to Rome; it is even later yet under the pontificate of Nicholas V., worthy precursor of Leo X., that we should date its organization, when he ordered it transferred to the Vatican.

With M. Blume we shall delay to 1468 the year of the founding of the *Marciana*, rather than taking it back, as is commonly done, to 1362, when Petrarch bequeathed his library to the Republic of Venice.

Le Prince, in his *Histoire de la Bibliothèque Royale de Paris*, states that several kings of France, before the XIV.th century, have had libraries but it appears that they subsisted only during the lifetime of these princes, each of whom disposed of his library at will in favor of whomever he judged appropriate. Almost invariably dispersed after their deaths, only those few books which had been used in their chapels passed on to their successors. The Louvre Library, whose catalogue its librarian Mallet drew up in 1373, contained 910 volumes at that time, a very considerable number given the ignorance of those days. During the misfortunes which befell the kingdom at the beginning of the reign of Charles VII., this library was entirely dispersed. The one which Louis XI. formed thereafter experienced the same fate. It is the year 1527 which is mostly agreed upon as the date of founding for the *Royal Library of Paris*. Francis I. started it at Fontainebleau and later assembled there those books which had belonged to the libraries of Blois and of the Lord High Constable of Bourbon. But its true founding must be brought up to 1595, the year Henry IV. had it transferred to Paris.

We have felt compelled to include the *Laurentian Library* despite the restricted number of its volumes, because of the worth of its holdings and the great fame of the library. Indeed, for a long time it passed for the richest in Europe and was one of the illustrious strongholds in the annals of literature. Moreover, a librarian-scholar who visited there recently considers the catalogue of its precious manuscripts as a masterpiece of method and criticism; and the reigning grand duke added a pavilion to the building which houses it to preserve in it the magnificent collection of incunabula which the Count of Elci had bequeathed to him. This collection is one of the most remarkable in existence particularly for the selection of its copies, by their perfect state of preservation and the richness of their bindings. We learn from a high personality that the copy of *Lucain*, published by the Count of Elci and which he ordered brought to Vienna did not cost less than 1,500 francs.

The desire to rectify certain erroneous opinions generally adopted as incontrovertible truths about the ignorance of the Turks and their alleged literary intolerance, despite the material facts published by MM. Toderini, Mouradja D'Ohsson, de Hammer, Jouannin and other great Orientalists to that effect, has caused us to include in the table the *Imperial Library* founded inside the Seraglio [i.e. the Sultan's Palace] by Hamed III. and opened by the Sultan with the greatest of solemnity in 1719. But we have not deemed it necessary to include in our table the *Library of Buda*, although founded in 1466 by Matthias Corvinus, because, after shining among the richest of Europe during the reign of that great Prince, it was entirely dispersed after his death, which occurred in 1490.

Chronological Table
of the founding of some of Europe's
most remarkable libraries

Heidelberg; the *Palatine*, in 1390; dispersed and sacked in 1623; revived in 1652; restored and augmented in 1816.

Rome; the *Vatican*, transported from Avignon to Rome in 1417 by Martin V.; considerably augmented and organized by Nicolas V. in 1447.

Regensburg; of the *Town*, in 1430.

Turin; of the *University*, in 1436; it was the private library of the dukes and of the kings until 1729; it is only since 1580 that it became considerable.

Vienna; *The Imperial*, in 1440; public since 1575.

Florence; the *Laurentian*, in 1444; almost dispersed in 1497; restored in 1500 and opened to the public in 1571.

Cesena; the *Malatestiana*, in 1452.

Venice; the *Marciana*, in 1468.

Oxford; the *Bodleian*, in 1480; public since 1602.

Copenhagen; of the *University*, in 1483.

Frankfurt-On-The-Main; of the *Town*, in 1484.

Marburg; of the *University*, in 1527.
Strasburg; in 1531.
Leipzig; of the *University*, in 1544.
Jena; of the *University*, in 1548.
Dresden; the *Royal*, in 1556.
Edinburgh; of the *University*, in 1580.
Leiden; of the *University*, in 1586.
Paris; the *Royal*, or *National*, in 1595.
Munich; the *Royal* or *Central*, in 1595.
Escorial; of the *Convent*, in 1596.
Wolfenbüttel; the *Ducal*, in 1604.
Milan; the *Ambrosian*, in 1609.
Lyon; in 1609.
Rome; the *Angelica*, in 1620.
Uppsala; of the *University*, in 1621.
Padua; of the *University*, in 1629.
Copenhagen; the *Royal*, in 1648.
Berlin; the *Royal*, in 1661.
Paris; the *Mazarin*, in 1661; public since 1688.
Gotha; the *Ducal*, in 1680.
Edinburgh; of the *Advocates*, in 1682.
Weimar; the *Grand ducal*, in 1691.
Madrid; the *Royal*, in 1712.
Florence; the *Magliabecchiana*, in 1714; open to the public in 1747.
Constantinople; the *Imperial Library*, inside the Seraglio, in 1719.
Bologna; of the *Unversity* or of the *Institute*, in 1725.
St. Petersburg; the *Imperial*, in 1728.
Goettingen; of the *Unversity*, 1736.
London; of the *British Museum*, or the *Royal*, in 1759.
Milan; of *Brera*, in 1763; open to the public in 1770.
Stuttgart; the *Royal*; founded in Ludwigsburg in 1765; transferred to
    Stuttgart in 1778.

II. Description of the Premises

The building occupied by the Imperial Library forms part of the palace of the Emperor, built by Charles VI. It runs along one full side of the square of Joseph, of which it constitutes the background and the main ornamental relief. The statue of Minerva, riding a triumphal chariot drawn by four horses, decorates the middle of the upper portion of the facade. On one side Atlas is represented, carrying the celestial sphere flanked by two figures embodying [the science of] astronomy; on the other side is Tellus holding up the terrestrial sphere, and [likewise flanked by] two figures representing [the science of] geometry.

The interior of this building, which has long since become too small to suitably hold the enormous mass of books which form the library, offers only eight rooms of very different dimensions, to wit:

The *great hall*, which has to be placed among the most magnificent in existence. It is a parallelogram of 246 Viennese feet in length by 45 in width and 62 in height; an oval dome of 92½ feet in height, supported by eight columns, forms its center. In the middle stands the equestrian statue of Charles VI. in marble from Carrara, surrounded by the statues of twelve other emperors of the House of Austria. The gold, the marble and the paint work are sometimes displayed profusely. A superb fresco of Daniel Gran decorates the ceiling of the dome: it represents all the sciences through allegorical figures joined in a circle holding hands. The cabinets crowned with large golden medallions, the vast gallery, which goes clear around the room and to which one gains access by four hidden stairways, are decorated with gildings; and, as in the case of the remaining woodwork, all of these are in a perfectly finished walnut.

Then come two *small rooms* destined for the manuscripts, a *tiny room* for the *incunabula*, or books printed since the invention of printing until 1500, a *room* for the *readers*, two small *offices* [and] an *anteroom*.

III. Successive Increases
of the Imperial Library

One could apply to the library what M. Ebert said, several years ago, about the one of Dresden, to wit that with the exception of bequests, gifts and family legacies, the mass of its books has never been augmented through plunder or violent incorporations (as was the case for quite a few other famous libraries) but always through legitimate purchases. We borrow from the interesting work of the Aulic Counselor, M. de Mosel, a few of the most remarkable acquisitions, which have most contributed to the formation of this library: they represent, so to speak, the main and most brilliant highlights of its long existence.

Chronological Table
of the Principal Acquisitions of the Imperial Library
of Vienna

Years	Acquisitions
1578	Purchase from the library of Sambucus for 2,500 ducats; it is claimed that it contained 2,618 volumes.
1636	Acquisition by legacy of the rich collection of books and of manuscripts of the librarian Tengnagel.
1655	Purchase of the library of Count Fugger of Augsburg for 15,000 florins; it contained 15,000 volumes estimated by scholars to be worth 80,000 florins, [expressed] in the value of those days.
1687	Purchase of the library of Lambecius for 2,300 florins; it contained 3,000 volumes and 200 precious manuscripts.
1674	Purchase of the library of Marquis Gabrega, composed of 2,498 volumes almost exlusively Spanish.

11

Years	*Acquisitions*
1720	Purchase of the library of Baron von Hohendorf for 60,000 florins; it contained 7,039 works and 252 superb manuscripts.
1724	Purchase of the library of His Grace Cardona, Archbishop of Valencia, in Spain, for 8,000 ducats; it contained approximately 4,000 choice volumes.
1738	Purchase of the library of Prince Eugene, for a life annuity of 10,000 florins paid to his heiress. This magnificent collection contained 15,000 volumes, 237 manuscripts, 290 volumes of prints in folio and 215 sketches.
1740 & 1741	Acquisition of 1,932 volumes of the collection of the librarian Garelli.
1762	Acquisition of 1,500 volumes coming from the private library of Emperor Francis I. who died at Innsbruck.
1768	Purchase, for 12,500 florins, of the Atlas of Baron von Stosch, consisting of 234 volumes in folio, containing close to 10,000 maps.
1780	Purchase of the library of the town of Vienna for the sum of 6,000 florins; it contained 5,037 volumes in print and 76 manuscripts; among the printed books were 351 incunabula.
1792-1835	Acquisition of a large number of very rare music scores of the XVI.th and XVIII.th centuries, transferred, upon the proposal of the Count of Dietrichstein, through his efforts, of a Imperial Chapel; also, formation, throught his efforts, of a well selected collection of about 8,000 autographs. Purchase of the best works published in Paris and of the luxury editions off the printing presses of V. Degen; for the acquisition of these very last items alone His Majesty the Emperor disbursed the sum of 10,575 florins. Acquisition through gift, of a large number of works of the highest importance and very expensive, such as the *Antiquities of Mexico* by Lord Kingsborough, and the large collection of the *Records* of England, printed at the expense of Parliament, among which was the famous *Domesday Book*, etc.

IV. Comparison of the Imperial Library with the Largest in Europe Before the Year 1789

But so that the reader may have a good notion of the distinguished place that this library has occupied for such a long time, we are going to offer him a table in which the number of its volumes stands compared to those [numbers] which the richest libraries now existing possessed at different times, and, even, to those of some [of the libraries] that have ceased to exist, although they shone brilliantly on the first rank of the most substantial ones of their time.

It is in the works already cited in the chronological table of the founding of the principal public libraries of Europe, and in others that we shall mention below, that we have drawn the information classed in the following one. Here we cite again *Brassiacus* and *Pflug*, *Schier* and *Vallaszky* as the sources consulted for everything that concerns the famous *Library of Matthias Corvinus*. Invoking their authority, we shall recall that this magnanimous Prince, a worthy emulator of the Medicis and of Francis I., spent no less that 30,000 ducats every year to build up the library he had founded in Buda under the direction of the Italians Galeotti and Ugoletti. This sum, taking into account the difference of the actual average value of a silver mark from 1466 to 1490, would be worth almost 165,000 ducats today. Valuing the latter at 11 francs apiece, we find the enormous sum of 1,815,000 francs annually disbursed by this Prince for the purchase of new books! One should even have to carry it to 4,840,000 francs if one were to subscribe to Schanz's opinion, who, adopting the authority of several Hungarian authors, cites 80,000 ducats as the sum spent annually for the purchase and copying [costs] of the books of this library. However enormous this last sum may appear, there are authentic facts one can draw from to demonstrate, if not its mathematical exactness, at least its probability. For instance, we know that it was composed almost exclusively of manuscripts; that it numbered about 55,000 volumes; that almost all of them were remarkable by the beauty of their characters and by their bindings adorned with gold and silver, which made their purchase much more expensive; that this Prince maintained numerous copyists in Rome, Florence and Venice, there to copy books for his library, and that he compensated richly several travelers to bring back Greek, Syrian, Arabic and Hebrew manuscripts for him from Constantinople and the main cities of the Orient, [books] which they had bought on his account at high price; that a few years after his death, the Medici of Florence claimed in 1498 from his successor, Wladislaw, 1,400 ducats for a *Bible* and 500 ducats for a *Bréviaire* that had been bought for him. Estimating the average price of each volume at only 35 ducats, which is a very modest sum, bearing in mind what we have just mentioned, we find that the 55,000 volumes would represent a sum of 1,925,000 ducats, and that this sum, spread over the 24 years of his reign, would give a mean expenditure of 80,204 ducats, a sum almost identical to that M. Schanz assigns to him. The then 1,925,000 ducats would represent today the enormous sum of 116,462,500 francs.

But one cannot speak about the magnificent Library of Matthias Corvinus without mentioning two other immense collections, which shared its lot. We mean the *Libraries* of *Queen Christina* and of *Antoine Manutius*. The first was formed in Stockholm by this famous Princess at enormous expense. At the time of its dispersion it must not have been much inferior to that of Buda, especially if we are to judge its importance by the large number of manuscripts which it possessed in 1653, then estimated to be 8,000; however, we shall relegate to the most ridiculous of exaggerations the 400,000 volumes which a voluminous geography, recently published in London, attributes to it. The rich library which *Antoine Manutius* had succeeded in gathering in Rome, also must have been very considerable, though we are quite far from sharing the opinion of a few estimable scholars, who, presently, relying on the vague assertions of a few authors—contemporaries of the famous typographer and man of letters of Venice—have stated that 80,000 was the number of its volumes.

It is useless to observe that the number of volumes existing in 1789 in the libraries included in the following table was, and could only be, approximate; such is the result of our research based upon the known number of volumes before and after that date. Therefore we have qualified these numbers with a question mark: it indicates our doubts. However, we are forced to justify the number of volumes which we have assigned to the *Library of Warsaw* and to those of *Munich* and of *Copenhagen*.

It is not according to common estimates, which are always exaggerated and very erroneous, that we shall grant, with estimable authors, 300,000 volumes to the *Zaluski Library* which, after the fall of Warsaw, Catherine II. forced the Prussians to hand over in order to decorate the capital of the Russian Empire with it. [Rather,] it is according to the information published in 1814 by Bentkowski in his history of Polish literature, whose communication we owe to one of the best living Slavicists, the famous M. Kopitar. This scholar gracefully translated for us the passage concerning this library; its holdings are estimated in it at 200,000 works only, of which 20,000 are Polish. Considering that in that number there must be a large quantity of theses, of brochures and of items of a transient nature, and that, moreover, it is not the result of a true enumeration but only of an approximate estimation, we feel that we would not digress too far from the truth if we brought it to 150,000 volumes for 1789.

It is common knowledge that the *Library of Munich* began to be considerable only toward the end of the XVIII.th century, and especially after the merging of the rich libraries of the convents, abbeys and ecclesiastical sovereignties, suppressed since 1789, of which several were among the oldest of Germany. All these large incorporations made it in a short time the second largest library of the world with respect to the number of volumes it contained.

As for the *Royal Library of Copenhagen*, we have estimated the number of its volumes, at that same time, according to its history, published in Danish by M. Wurlaff, in 1825, whose translation, with respect to its richness, we owe to the kindness of M. de Geway, one of the assistant librarians of the Imperial Library.

We still have to justify the large-sized modification which we have brought to the evaluation of the illustrious Van-Swieten, who, in 1787, carried the number of volumes of the *Imperial Library*, whose administrator he was, to 250,000. Knowing rather precisely the number of volumes it possesses presently, and being able to evaluate rather exactly its average annual increases from 1787 to 1835, it was not too difficult for us to approximate the number of volumes it contained at that time. Our calculations yielded us only 210,000, a number which we have adopted, despite the categorical assertions of Van-Swieten and all the authority carried by his name.

Comparative Table
of the Riches of the Main Libraries of Europe
at Various Times

| *Years* | *Number of printed volumes and of the manuscripts* |

Imperial Library in Vienna
1663   90,000 volumes, and more than 10,000 manuscripts.
1789   196,000 volumes, and nearly 14,000 manuscripts.

Royal Library in Paris
1660   1,435 printed volumes.
1661   16,746 volumes and manuscripts; this large increase was due to the bequest of Dupuis.
1669   30,000 volumes.
1683   40,000 volumes and 10,542 manuscripts.
1715   70,000 volumes.
1789   149,000 ? volumes.

Library of St. Germain, near Paris
1789   100,000 volumes and 20,000 manuscripts.

Mazarin Library in Paris
1644   12,000 volumes.
1651   37,880 volumes.
1789   45,000 ? volumes.

Vatican Library in Rome
1455   5,000 manuscripts.
1685   25,000 ? volumes and 16,000 manuscripts.
1789   40,000 ? volumes and 32,000 ? manuscripts.

Barberini Library in Rome
1664   40,000 volumes and 6,000 manuscripts.
1789   50,000 ? volumes and 6,000 manuscripts.

Library of Matthias Corvinus in Buda
1490*   55,000 volumes.

*Date of his death.

Years   *Number of printed volumes*
                              and of the manuscripts

Royal Library of Dresden
1574   1,721 volumes.
1580   2,354 volumes.
1595   16,000 ? volumes (5,668 works).
1771   174,000 volumes.
1789   190,000 ? volumes.

Royal Library in Berlin
1687   20,600 volumes and 1,618 manuscripts.
1715   50,000 volumes.
1735   62,990 volumes.
1740   more than 72,000 volumes and 2,000 manuscripts.
1789   160,000 ? volumes.

Ambrosian Library in Milan
1644   30,000 volumes and 9,000 manuscripts.
1685   38,000 volumes and 9,500 manuscripts.
1729   45,000 volumes.
1789   55,000 ? volumes and 12,000 ? manuscripts.

Bodleian Library in Oxford
1789   125,000 ? volumes.

Royal Library in Copenhagen
1786   100,000 volumes, according to Ekkart cited by Wurlaff.
1789   140,000 ? volumes.

Imperial Library in St. Petersburg
1789   130,000 ? volumes.

Royal Library in Munich
1789   110,000 ? volumes.

University Library in Bologna
1789   110,000 ? volumes.

Zaluski Library in Warsaw
1789   150,000 ? volumes.

Years   *Number of printed volumes*
                                   and of the manuscripts

University Library in Goettingen
1789   160,000 ? volumes.

Ducal Library in Wolfenbüttel
1789   100,000 ? volumes.

Upon simple inspection of this table one sees the eminent
position occupied for such a long time by the Imperial Library. Indeed,
the number of its volumes, independently of their great value, was
double, triple and even more than quadruple that of several other
libraries, which none the less were ranked among the main ones of
Europe. This material richness and the advantage of having almost
consistently counted its librarians among famous scholars brought
upon it the great fame it has so rightly enjoyed. Since 1789, the
numerous suppressions of convents, abbeys and ecclesiastical
sovereignties as well as the political upheavals which befell several
countries have powerfully contributed to the dramatic increase of
several libraries, have led to the creation of other entirely new ones,
and have displaced the one of Vienna from the high position it had
occupied for nearly three centuries. All the facts we were able to collect
on this subject, with those we have classified in the preceding table,
authorize us to consider the Imperial Library as *the largest and richest
of Europe*, and, *consequently, of the world*, until the French Revolution, a date forever committed to the memory of mankind. We shall
see below which libraries have surpassed it since, and which one must
today be considered as the largest ever to have existed.

V. Statistics of the Imperial Library

But it is time to offer the reader a brief glimpse of the principal parts which constitute the literary treasures preserved in the Imperial Library. We shall outline it with those documents which we owe to the courteousness of its scholarly historian, and with the equally important information that M. Kopitar furnished us on the *manuscripts* and the *incunabula*, and M. Lechner on the *printed books*.

M. de Mosel classifies the literary riches of the Library of which he is the head librarian in the following manner:

1. Rare Items (*Cimelia*)

They number twenty-four, of which the principal ones are:

A bronze tablet, containing the *Senatus consultum de Bacchanalibus*, of the year of Rome 567, or of 186 B.C.

Tabula Peutingeriana, on vellum; it is the *road map* of the Roman Empire of the IV.th century, copied in the XIII.th, and found by Conr[ad] Celtis, a German scholar, who died in 1508 in Vienna, sold by him to Senator Peutinger of Augsburg; Prince Eugene of Savoy bought it in 1717, while he was in the Semlin encampment. It is a priceless item of ancient geography. The first folio, which pictures a part of Africa, Spain and England, was lacking from the beginning; this means that even Celtis did not possess it. Professor, M. Wyttenbach has just discovered a portion of it in the binding of an incunabulum of the library of Trier: it is the middle portion, which represents a large part of Spain.

T. Livii Decas V., *unique* manuscript, long ago brought from Scotland by Saint *Suitbertus*, Apostle of the Frisians. It is according to this manuscript that a large part [of the work] of this great historian of Padua has been published.

Sancti Hilarii de Trinitate, on papyrus, manuscript of the IV.th century.

19

Psalterium Davidis, which belonged to Charlemagne, in gold letters (*Codex aureus*).

Grammatici Bobienses, on palimpsests, coming from the same monastery of Bobbio from which those, which the Ambrosian Library of Milan, of the Vatican in Rome, and those of Torino and Naples possess, originated. They are now printing unpublished ones in Vienna.

Charta Ravennas et Pieria, documents of sales and of gifts in Lombardic style of writing, called *longobardica*, on papyrus, of the V.th century, published by Montfaucon and Maffei.

A roll of *Mexican hieroglyphs*; it is a monument of the ancient Mexicans, consisting of a long skin covered with hieroglyphs painted in colors, recently published by Lord Kingsborough in his *Antiquities of Mexico*, of which it is the outstanding item.

Prayer books, ornamented with miniatures, manuscripts coming from the *Library of Matthias Corvinus*, richly mounted and whose most ornate is the *Philostrate*, translated from the Greek by Bonfinius. Besides, the manuscripts copied for Corvinus are more beautiful than they are any good.

2. The Manuscripts

They number 16,016, of which 2,789 are on parchment and 2,634 on paper, before the invention of printing. Among the manuscripts subsequent to this memorable discovery, 8,523 are on paper. In addition, there are 985 Greek manuscripts, 85 Hebrew ones and 1,000 Oriental ones. The 723 Chinese and Indian books have been classified as manuscripts.

Among the rarest manuscripts, we shall restrict ourselves to citing the following ones, in addition to those that we already mentioned among the "Rare Items."

Among the Greek manuscripts we shall mention at least:

The *Dioscoride*; it is upon the order of Princess *Juliana Anicia*, only daughter of Emperor *Olybrius*, that it was written, in the V.th century, in uncial lettering and with paintings showing medicinal plants. At its end are unpublished fragments by Doctor Cratevas. M. *Weigel*, learned physician from Dresden, has taken variants and copies from it. The Library owes this important acquisition with more than 300 other Greek manuscripts to Busbecke, Austrian ambassador to Constantinople around 1550. It is only much later that Frenchmen and Englishmen have drawn [information] from this same source.

Another *Dioscoride*, similar and almost as ancient, brought from Naples.

Nicephori Callisti hist. eccl. of the X.th century; it is a *unique* manuscript, which was used for the first edition of this work.

Fragmens de la Génèse, in silver uncials on royal vellum, decorated with beautiful drawings; the last ones were first published by Lambecius in his catalogue and recently by Dibdin in his bibliographical voyage.

A *fragment* on papyrus *du III. Concile de Constantinople* of the year 680–681.

Nouveau Testament in Greek, of the XIII.th century; Erasmus consulted it for his second edition of the New Testament, and he wrote in his own hand the usage he made of this manuscript.

We shall add that several other precious Greek manuscripts of the Imperial Library were used in the first editions of more than one work, such as the *Plotinus*, the *Chrysostome* of Savilius, the *Demosthenes* of Taylor, etc.

Among the German manuscripts we shall cite:

Paraphrase des Pseaumes by *Notker*, a Benedictine monk of the X.th century, the best ancient prose writer (Old High German).

Ottfridi Messias, work in verse about the Gospels, of the IX.th century. M. *Graff* has just again used this manuscript for publication in Berlin, under the title *Krist*.

Codex Clathratus. They are fragments of the oldest German translation of the Gospel of St. Matthew, from the beginning of the VIII.th century, coming from the scraps of paper in ancient bindings. Librarians have been eagerly publishing them, thereby fulfilling the wishes of the great grammarian Grimm.

Bible Allemande, written in the XIV.th century for Emperor Wenceslas, decorated with superb miniatures. It forms 6 vol. in folio.

A manuscript on paper in folio, with 245 word engravings, from *Hans Burgmaier*, with the title of *Weyss Khunig*, containing the history of the life of Emperor Frederick III. (V.) and of his son, Maximilian I.; another manuscript, written in the year 1512, on paper, in folio, containing several details of the life of Emperor Maximilian I.; etc.

Among the French manuscripts, we shall cite only:

Old novels with miniatures, among which the one of *Gérard de Roussillon* is the most unusual; then a *Bréviaire d'Amour*, or poems in Provençal language. A manuscript in parchment, in folio, written in round letters and in old orthography, with very ornate miniatures in gothic style, containing *l'histoire du chevalier' Tristan* or *Tristram de la table ronde*; its date is not certain, but it goes assuredly back to the XIV.th century at least.

3. The Incunabula

Books printed during the XV.th century are called by that name; the Library does not possess less than 12,000 of them, inclusive of more than 3,000 duplicates; they are housed in the so-called room of *Incunabula*. Among the most remarkable we shall cite:

Apuleji Opera. Romae [Rome], Conr[ad] Schweynheym and Arn[old] Pannartz, 1469, fol. in membrana.

Auli Gellii, Noctes Atticae. Romae, Schweynheym and Pannartz; 1469, fol. in membrana.

Sancti Hieronymi Epistolae, 2 vol. in folio; Romae, Schweynheym and Pannartz, 1468.

Julii Caesaris Commentarii, one vol. in folio; Romae, 1469. We shall observe that only the *Tite-Live* of Sykes, extant in London, is lacking to complete the five, [and only five,] unique incunabula on parchment printed by Pannartz in Rome.

Psalmorum Codex, Mog[untiae, i.e. Mainz], Joh[ann] Fust and Petrus Schoiffer of Gernsheim, 1457 in vig. assumpt. fol. goth. in membrana.

Duranti (Guilielmi) *Rationale divinorum officiorum.* Mog[untiae], Joh[ann] Fust and Petrus Schoiffer of Gernsheim; 1459, sixth day of October; fol. goth. in membrana.

Clementis Papae V. Constitutionum Codex with ornamentation by the Reverend Father Joa[nnes] Andr[eus], Bishop of Aleria [Corsica]. Mog[untiae], Joh[ann] Fust and Petrus Schoiffer of Gernsheim; 1460, XXV. day of the month of June, fol. goth. in membrana.

Biblia latina. Moguntiae, Joh[ann] Fust and Petrus Schoiffer of Gernsheim; 1462; in vigilia assumptionis, fol. goth. in membrana.

Decretalium liber VI. Bonifacii VIII. Papae, with ornamentation. Mog[untiae] Joan[nes] Fust and Petrus Schoiffer of Gernsheim; 1465, XVII. day of the month of December, fol. goth. in membrana.

Lactantii Firmiani opera, in the monastery of Subiaco. Schweynheym and Pannartz; 1465, the last day but two of the month of October; fol.

Aquinatis (Thomae) II. Pars II. Partis Summae theol. Moguntiae. Petrus Schoiffer of Gernsheim; 1467, sixth day of the month of March, in fol. in membrana.

Aquinatis (Thomae) Opus quarti scripti. Moguntiae, Petrus Schoiffer; 1469, XIII.th of June, fol. goth. in membrana.

Justiniani Institutiones, with ornamentations of Joann[es] Andreae. Moguntiae. Petrus Schoiffer de G. 1468; 24th day of the month of May; fol. goth. in membrana.

Plinii Caec. Secundi Historia naturalis. Venet [Venice]. Vindelin de Spira, 1469; fol., in membrana.

Petrarca. Opere. Venet. Vindelinus de Spira; 1470. 4°.

Martialis epigrammata. Venet. Vendelin de Spira, c. 1470. 4°.

Plinii Caec. libri XXXVII. Venet. Nic[olas] Jenson; 1472; fol. in membrana.

Decretalium Gregorii Papae IX. new compilation, with ordinary words [characters] of M. Bernhard. Mog[untiae], Petrus Schoiffer of G., 1473. IX.th kal. of December, fol. goth. in membranis et in charta.

Bullae Aurea, germanice, Ulm. Leonhardi Holbein; 1484 fol. goth. in membrana.

It will be curious at this point to find here a few examples of the excessive prices to which the first editions have risen today. We shall borrow them from the scholarly work of M. Petit-Radel.

The *Bible*, so-called *"without date,"* 2 vol. in folio was paid 2,499 francs.

The *Commentaires de César*, edition of 1469, 1 vol. in fol. 1,362 fr.

The *Dante*, printed at Foligno in 1472; 1 vol. in 4°. 799 fr.

The *Florus*, printed at the Sorbonne, ca. 1470, 1 vol. in 8°. 801 fr.

The *Aulugelle*, printed in Rome in 1469; 1 vol. in folio. 1,760 fr.

The *Martial*, printed in Venice in 1470; 1 vol. in 8°. 1,274 fr.

The *Pline*, printed in Venice in 1469; 1 vol. in folio. 3,000 fr.

Total: 11,495 francs.

"A library put together in this fashion," says M. Petit-Radel, "would contain only seven books and would cost at least — because these prices increase forever — 11,495 francs. What would this be if one were to add only one volume such as the *Psautier* dated of 1457, which Louis XVIII. had acquired for the public library and for which the price rose to 12,000 francs?" We shall add that the *Decamerone* of Boccaccio, printed by Valdarfer in Venice, was sold in London, in 1812, for 2,260 pounds sterling, equivalent to 56,500 francs. This book was resold in 1819 for 918 [pounds sterling] or 22,950 francs. One can induce therefrom, but following a decreasing progression, for many more ordinary editions, what the price of the magnificent collection of 12,000 incunabula, which form that part of the Imperial Library, would be. However, it must be granted that for several years now bibliomania has been depressed a little, and that the price of first editions has decreased considerably; but that price is still quite high enough to let these 12,000 volumes represent an enormous sum.

4. The Printed Books
from the beginning of the XIV.th century
until the present

Their exact number is not known. According to the research that has just been concluded, and whose results we are indebted for to the kindness of the Count of Dietrichstein, the volumes would number approximately 230,000. In this number are included 30,000 theses, 30,000 brochures and fugitive pieces, transient items, and 6,000 folders of works which have not as yet been finished, forming a total of 66,000 items which, as we shall see below, could be counted as 10,000 volumes. We shall observe that in the 230,000 volumes there are more than 40,000 works, which, being bound with others in the same volumes, would, if they were separated from them, as is the custom in the larger percentage of the libraries, form another 40,000 to be added to these 230,000. Without any exaggeration, it can therefore be stated that the total number of volumes printed since the XVI.th century and preserved [in the Library] is 270,000.

5. The Collection of Prints

It is one of the largest and most important in existence. It is composed of 473 volumes in large folio, 510 volumes of different formats, 14 portfolios and 245 sketches in folio. All the works of all the famous Italian, German, Belgian, Dutch, French and English chalco-graphers and the huge *Atlas* of *Le Bleau*, a unique specimen on account of [its containing] 302 original drawings of the most renowned Dutch masters. It is Prince Eugene of Savoy who started this collection; it cost him 500,000 French *écus* [crowns]. In 1818 it constituted five-sixths of the whole collection extant in the Imperial Library. The scholar Bartsch, who was its director, valued it then at 3,000,000 florins in silver, equivalent to 7,500,000 francs. His calculations were based on the original price of Prince Eugene's collection and on the increase in value which prints have since experienced. The nature of this work does not even permit us to mention only the most remarkable items. We shall limit ourselves to stating that the number of items contained in this superb collection is estimated at 300,000. Here are a few numerical data which should help the reader in assigning a place to this collection among the most considerable public collections of Europe. The figures, which we have considered for the little table below, are and can only be approximate, and we are quite far from being able to guarantee their exactness on account of the great divergence of the many estimations which travelers and iconographers alike have given us:

Comparative Table
of the Principle Public Collections of Prints

Names of the Collections	Number of Items	
Paris (in the *Cabinet of Prints*)	more than	1,400,000
Munich	more than	300,000
Vienna	about	300,000
Dresden	about	250,000
London (in the *British Museum*)	about	100,000
Copenhagen	about	80,000
Amsterdam	almost	70,000

6. The Music Collection

This superb collection includes more than 6,000 volumes of theoretical and practical works. Among the former are several rare incunabula. Among the later are compositions by the most famous masters from the XV.th century to date. We shall mention, as curios, several compositions by the Emperors Ferdinand III., Leopold I. and Charles VI.

7. The Collection of Autographs

Although this collection began only a few years ago, as we have indicated on page 12, it already includes close to 8,000 items. It is divided into five main classifications, to wit: *Monarchs* and *princes*; *Ministers* and *statesmen*; *Generals* and *great captains*; *scholars, poets* and *men of letters*; *artists*.

Statistical Synopsis
of the Imperial Library

In summing up what we have just said about the different parts which compose the literary riches of this establishment, it can be seen that the Imperial Library presently counts:

> 270,000 volumes printed since 1500;
> 12,000 volumes of incunabula;
> 16,016 manuscripts;
> 1,242 volumes, portfolios and sketches, forming the collection of prints;

Total   299,258, or in round numbers, 300,000 volumes.

VI. Endowment and Personnel

For a long time the Library has been endowed with a considerable annual income, destined exclusively to the purchase of new books, prints, journals, etc., and binding costs. Since 1820 His Majesty the Emperor has even increased it to 19,000 silver florins, equivalent to 47,500 francs. However, should some extraordinary circumstance arise whereby rare or essential works could be obtained to augment the holdings of the Library, the administrator asks for the permission to acquire them: this authorization has not as yet been refused.

We shall not speak of the activity and zeal displayed for the improvement and the prosperity of this establishment by its present administrator, the Count of Dietrichstein: it is a fact known by all and on which everyone agrees. We shall only add that this noble lord, by his extreme affability and especially by his diversified knowledge, appears to us more qualified to direct a large public library than a goodly number of scholars, who, through special studies and their penchant for rare editions, use, to the detriment of studious people, for the purchase of works of at least very doubtful usefulness, the sums which the liberality of sovereigns and governments destine every year to the maintaining of public libraries, as much as possible, on a par with the rapid progress achieved these days by all the truly useful branches of human knowledge. Consequently, we have found in this establishment entrusted to his care books on history, geography, statistics, travel and political economy recently published in the most distant countries, books that we would have been looking for in vain in more than one large public library, though very renowned for the mass and the high price of their books but where they would only have had to offer us most of the masterpieces on ancient and modern typography and all the novelties concerning the fine arts and literature per se rather than the scientific works that we would have requested.

By the use of its endowment and by the legal deposit of one copy of all the publications which appear anywhere in the Austrian Empire, the mass of printed books increases yearly by 3,500 to 3,800 volumes, not to mention about 3,000 transient items, theses, calendars, prayer books, etc., which are not carried in the catalogue. This considerable yearly increase multiplies the difficulties of the librarians, who, for some years now, did not know where to put the books. The Count of Dietrichstein, in order to remedy, temporarily and in part, this inconvenience, to segregate the luxury works from the mass of general books, and to protect them against dust and humidity, ordered some large containers built: they were placed in two rows in the Large Room. But these large boxes spoil the beauty of this magnificent place without entirely serving the intended purpose. We shall even take the liberty of making a remark that the lack of space, which can be noted in virtually every large establishment of the capital of Austria, is, however, nowhere so strongly felt, nor so harmful, as here. We have seen on a large number of bookshelves that the books were placed on two and even three rows in depth: this makes their research very difficult and exposes them to easier damage. It would also be desirable that this magnificent establishment should finally possess a catalogue arranged by subject matter, following the method employed for the catalogue editions of the library of Goettingen and of the private library of Emperor Francis I.

Here are some numerical data with which the reader will be able to compare the endowment of the Imperial Library to that enjoyed by a few other well-known libraries. To simplify the elements of the small table which we have drawn up for them, we shall remark that according to the author of the *History of the University of Oxford*, already cited, the endowment of the Bodleian Library has been only 400 pounds sterling for the period 1780–1814, equivalent to 10,000 francs; that the endowment of the Royal Library of Berlin, according to M. Wilken, was only 500 thaler, or 1,855 francs, from 1795 to 1800; and that the vague assertions of our correspondent regarding the value of currencies renders as doubtful the reduction in francs of the endowment of the Royal Library of Copenhagen. We regret not having the means to enable us to indicate exactly the sum used yearly by the Royal Library of Paris for the purchase of new books and for binding; it should, however, be quite considerable because we do know that the sole endowment of the Cabinet of Prints is 15,000 francs.

We shall remind the reader that M. *Van-Praet*, who is the Head Librarian of the Printed Matters of the Royal Library in Paris, who is so esteemed for his vast erudition, for his prodigious memory and his complete abnegation for all those who so often have the opportunity to have recourse to his knowledge, has only 6,000 francs for salary, and housing in the Library complex; the salary of the scholar Ebert, former head of the Royal Library in Dresden, only 1,000 thalers.

Comparative Table
of the Annual Endowment of a Few Libraries

Names of the Libraries	*Annual Allocation in Francs*
Bodleian in Oxford	75,000
Imperial in Vienna	47,500
Royal in Berlin	29,680
Advocates in Edinburgh	25,000
Royal in Copenhagen	22,640
Of the *University* in Goettingen	20,000
Royal in Madrid	14,000
Of the *University* in Bologna	10,385
Royal in Dresden	10,000
Of the *Municipal* in Paris	8,000
Of *Brera* in Milan	5,000
Of the *University* in Pavia	5,000
Of the *University* in Padua	5,000
Marciana in Venice	5,000
Of the *University* in Vienna	3,750
Of the *Polytechnic Institute* in Vienna	3,000–3,750

The personnel of the Imperial Library includes thirteen persons whose titles and salaries are indicated in the following table:

Title of the Employees	*Salaries in* Florins	*Salaries in* Francs
An *Administrator* with salary of	5,000	12,500
A *Head Librarian,* having the rank of Aulic Counselor.	4,000	10,000
The *2nd Librarian*	2,000	5,000
The *3rd Librarian*	1,400	3,500
The *4th Librarian*	1,000	2,500
The *1st Assistant Librarian*	900	2,250
The *2nd Assistant Librarian*	800	2,000
The *3rd Assistant Librarian*	700	1,750
The *4th Assistant Librarian*	600	1,500
One *Candidate*	400	1,000
Three *messenger boys* having each a salary of	240	600

VII. Difficulties Encountered in the Statistical Comparison of Libraries

We have seen the eminent place that the Imperial Library has occupied until 1789. Let us now examine the rank we can assign to it among the largest libraries of the world. Because this comparison can solely be made in consideration of the number of its volumes when compared to those of the volumes of the largest collections of this type, we feel compelled to lead off the presentation of the comparative table we have drawn up for them with a few observations not only regarding the difficulties that even an approximate determination of the number of volumes of the principal libraries presents, but also regarding the very suitability of basing this comparison on the number of their volumes. We borrow them from our *Essai statistique sur les Bibliothèques de l'Ancien et du Nouveau Monde*, which we intend to publish at once.

In this work we state that we are not deluding ourselves, to wit, that even should the comparative table that we present reflect the exact number of volumes extant in each library, this would only be very secondary in importance and not at all sufficient to formulate a valid opinion about the respective importance of these establishments. Indeed, it is neither according to *format*, nor according to *number* of volumes that it can be measured. Two or three thousand volumes kept in the *War Depot* in Paris or in the *Military Archives* in Vienna, a few hundred precious manuscripts of the libraries — *Vatican* in Rome, *Laurentian* in Florence, *Ambrosian* in Milan, *Royal* in Paris, *Bodleian* in Oxford — or even only a thousand of the incunabula that these same libraries possess, or those of the other capitals of Europe, a thousand even of those which form the main part of the magnificent collection of Lord Spencer, rightly considered as the first of all the private libraries possessed today by individuals, any of these is without a doubt equivalent, from the scientific point of view as by their special nature or by their high price, to such and such library of Italy, of Spain or of Portugal, rich from 20,000 to 30,000 volumes, which treat solely

30

ascetic subjects, scholastic theology or ancient Aristotelian philosophy. How many thousands of these same volumes would not have to be gathered in order to represent only the value of a few of the portfolios which form the magnificent *collections of prints* of *His Majesty the Emperor of Austria*, of *His Imperial Highness the Archduke Charles*, and the *print rooms* annexed to the *libraries—Royal* of *Paris*, of *Munich*, of *Dresden*, of *London*, of *Amsterdam*, of *Copenhagen* and of the *Imperial Library* of Vienna! How many would not have to be collected to represent the value of a few small *special libraries*, for instance of the *libraries* of the illustrious Orientalists *Morrison*, *Klaproth, Neumann* and *de Hammer*, of that which the famous Baron *Schilling* gathered during his voyage to Kiachta, and which the scholars desire to see included in the library of some public establishment in St. Petersburg, where it is at present; or yet of the previous *botanical library* of *M. Decandolle* in Geneva, joined with the magnificent herbarium of this first of living botanists; or even of the *collection of Japanese books*, which the famous traveler *Siebold* has just brought to Europe, a collection, which, despite its scantiness, being only 1,500 volumes in size, is the largest that this part of the world possesses, independently of the importance of the works themselves!

But while we are admitting the inadequacy of this isolated element when applied to measure the relative importance of libraries, we do nonetheless persist in always considering it as the first basis for any comparison to which these establishments could be subjected. We state even that it is, as yet, the only element which is translatable in figures. Considering that in this work we relate only the principal libraries, whose generality or speciality is evoked by their title or by the name of the establishment to which they belong, the discriminating reader could never run the risk of confusing libraries composed on a very large scale or almost exclusively of modern works, or at least important enough with respect to the sciences, literature or fine arts, with similar collections formed long ago in the peaceful retreats of certain religious corporations — collections, which, today, have lost almost all the value they once possessed. Forewarned by these considerations, the intelligent reader will never establish a comparison between elements which would not be comparable. Therefore, their number of volumes will represent to a certain point their respective relative importance. Besides, this element is the only one that travelers, historians and statisticians have gone to the trouble to register to date; it is also the only one which permits us to make useful and interest-generating comparisons, of an approximate nature, between the present era, so rich in achievements of the human mind, and those eras which have preceded it.

Frankly stated, we can say without fear of erring, that, with the exception of a few of the principal libraries of Europe, we still do not know the number of volumes each one of these useful establishments possesses, establishments so numerous today in this part of the world and still so rare in America, the United States alone excepted. The long and varied studies which we have undertaken during the preparation of the *Tableau comparatif* of the principal public libraries of Europe, published in 1822 in the *Essai Statistique sur le Royaume de Portugal** and the *Résumé Statistique,* concerning the principal public libraries of Europe and of America, which we have published in 1828,† have yielded us a mass of facts as interesting as important, which support our assertion. The imposing and minute details, so frequently published by the statisticians, the geographers and the travelers offer only an illusory exactness because contemporary authors, writing practically in the very same year, assign to the same library numbers of volumes which differ from one another by a fourth, a third, half, and even more than fourfold and tenfold!

The following table is only a fraction of the one we have drawn up for our handwritten thesis. It shows the stunning disparity of estimations proffered on the number of volumes contained in the same library by the most outstanding geographers, by the most scholarly statisticians and by the most discriminating travelers, as well as the opinions emitted by a few of these clever men of letters, who are consummate in the art of usurping the works of their predecessors without having the tactfulness of giving them credit by naming them.

We greatly regret not to be able to include in the table of the libraries of Paris the estimations drawn from the excellent *Statistique de la France* from 1818 to 1828, a work which a hard-working scholar, M. Bottin, publishes every year with important improvements under the modest title of *Almanach du Commerce.* These data would certainly increase the significance of the reconciliation of the figures describing the riches of the libraries of the capital of France. We do not cite his evaluations after 1828 because, having worked with this scholar, we would be including our own figures rather than intercalating his estimations on these same libraries.

---

*Essai Statistique sur le Royaume de Portugal et d'Algarve comparé aux autres Etats de l'Europe, et suivi d'un coup d'oeil sur l'état actuel des sciences, des lettres et des beaux-arts parmi les Portugais des deux Hemisphères. *Paris, chez Rey et Gravier, 2 gros vol. in 8. 1822. Prix, 16 francs.*

†La Monarchie Française en 1828 comparée aux principaux Etats du Monde. *Paris 1828, chez Jules Renouard; un tableau in plano. Prix, 6 francs.*

Comparative Table
of the principal opinions emitted on the number of volumes
of a few famous libraries

Authors	Volumes	Number of Manuscripts	Theses, brochures, fugitive items, etc.
Paris **Royal Library**			
Ebert	350,000	70,000	
Petit-Radel	350,000	50,000	and 350,000
Boismarsas	350,000	50,000	350,000
La *Revue Britannique* (1827)	450,000	80,000	450,000
Bailly	450,000	80,000	450,000
Villenave	450,000	100,000	and more than 400,000
Malchus	500,000	50,000	
Schnabel	500,000 to 900,000	80,000	
Bisinger	800,000	50,000	
André*	800,000	50,000	
Mazarin Library			
Petit-Radel	90,000	3,437	
Malchus	90,000	3,437	
Bailly	100,000	4,000	
Villenave	100,000	4,000	
Boismarsas	150,000	4,000	
Municipal Library			
Petit-Radel	15,000		
Boismarsas	15,000		
Bailly	45,000		
Villenave	45,000		
Madrid **Royal Library**			
Villenave	100,000	a large number	
Ebert	100,000	2,000	
Haendel†	125,000		
Langlois§	130,000		
Hassel	130,000	2,000	
Hassel**	180,000		
Moreau de Jonnès	200,000		
Malchus	200,000	2,000	
La *Revue Britannique* (1827)	more than 200,000	a large number	
Bailly (1833)††	more than 200,000	a large number	

Citing the Journal de la Librairie.
†*Citing Laborde.*
§*Citing Mignano.*
**Citing other authors.*
††*In the* Journal de la Société française de Statistique Universelle.

Authors	Volumes	Number of Manuscripts	Theses, brochures, fugitive items, etc.
Escorial Convent Library			
Bisinger	--	60,000*	
Ebert	17,800	4,300	
Laborde	30,000		
Stein	60,000		
Hassel	90,000		
Malchus	90,000	a large number	
La *Revue Britannique* (1827)	130,000	4,300	
Bailly (1833)†	130,000	4,300	
Villenave§	130,000	5,000	
Moreau de Jonnès	130,000	15,000	
Rome Vatican Library			
Schnabel	30,000	4,000	
Blume	30,000	25,000	
Ebert	30,000	40,000	
Villenave	30,000	40,000	
André	40,000	40,000	
Valery	80,000	24,000	
Rampoldi	90,000	and more than 45,000	
Malchus	160,000		
Bisinger	160,000		
La *Revue Britannique* (1827)	400,000	50,000	
Bailly (1833)**	400,000	50,000	
D'Haussez	800,000	38,000	
Eustace	from 200,000–1,000,000	50,000	
Quarterly Review (1826)††			
Florence Magliabecchian Library			
Malchus	90,000		
Blume	100,000	8,000	
Hassel	120,000		
Ebert	120,000	8,000-9,000	
Amati	more than 150,000		
La Guida di Firenze	150,000	10,000	
Valery	150,000	12,000	
Laurentian Library			
André	150,000	more than 5,000	

*Observing that they are Arabic and Oriental manuscripts.
†In the Journal de la Société française de Statistique Universelle.
§Observing that it is the largest of the peninsula, and one of the world's richest!
**In the Journal de la Société française de Statistique Universelle.
††The anonymous author of this article claims that it is the most considerable one in the world!

Authors	Volumes	Number of Manuscripts	Theses, brochures, fugitive items, etc.
Blume	150,000	6,000	
Ebert	150,000	8,000	
Valery	150,000	9,000	
Hassel	20,000*		
Villenave	90,000	3,000	
La *Revue Britannique* (1827)	90,000	about 3,000	
Bailly (1833)†	90,000	3,000	
Malchus	120,000		

Naples
Library of the Borbonica Museum

Bisinger	80,000		
Hassel	80,000		
Malchus	80,000		
Ebert	80,000	4,000	
Villenave	80,000	4,000	
Valery	150,000	3,000	
Galanti	more than 150,000	3,000	
André	160,000		
Umili	180,000		

Bologna
University Library

Valery	80,000	4,000	
André	more than 100,000		
Rampoldi	more than 100,000	a large number	
L'Abbé Andres (1780)	110,000		
Lalande	115,000		
The Librarian, M. Ferrucci	120,000		
Bisinger	150,000		
Ebert	150,000		
Malchus	160,000		
Blume	200,000		
Conversations-Lexikon	200,000		
Modern Traveller	200,000		

Milan
Brera Library

Valery	100,000		
Ebert	120,000	many	
Malchus	140,000		

We shall remind the reader that this evaluation and the following ones could not be more erroneous since this library contains exclusively manuscripts. It is only since the recent donation of Count d'Elci that it also contains printed books; but they are only incunabula. We have already commented on the full importance of this precious collection on pages 7–8.

†*In the* Journal de la Société française de Statistique Universelle.

Authors	Volumes	Number of Manuscripts	Theses, brochures, fugitive items, etc.
The Librarian, M. Gironi	169,000	a thousand	
Rampoldi	almost 200,000		
Ambrosian Library			
Gironi	40,000	14,000	
Bailly (1833)*	more than 46,000	12,000	
Blume	50,000	10,000	
Villenave	50,000	12,000	
Valery	60,000	10,000	
Ebert	60,000	15,000	
Malchus	76,000	15,000	
Hassel	90,000	15,000	
Bisinger	90,000	15,000	
Amati	more than 100,000†		
Millin	140,000		
Turin University Library			
D'Haussez	35,000 to 40,000		
Hassel	60,000		
Rampoldi	60,000§		
Amati	110,000		
Valery	112,000	1,980	
Malchus	120,000		
Berlin Royal Library			
Schnabel	140,000	7,000	
Hassel	160,000		
Malchus	160,000		
Bisinger	160,000		
La *Revue Britannique* (1827)	160,000		
Bailly (1833)**	160,000		
André	160,000	7,000	
Guthrie by Langlois	180,000		
Amati	190,000		
Ebert	200,000	2,000	
Villenave	200,000	2,000	
Schubert	220,000		
Wachler	250,000	4,611	
Wilken	250,000	4,611	
Zedlitz	300,000 to 400,000	more than 7,000	

*In the Journal de la Société française de Statistique Universelle.
†M. Amati observes that in that number are included 4,633 volumes containing 18,000 manuscripts.
§This is the number of the printed books only.
**In the Journal de la Société française de Statistique Universelle.

Authors	Volumes	Number of Manuscripts	Theses, brochures, fugitive items, etc.
Dresden			
Royal Library			
Schnabel	200,000	5,000	
Ebert	220,000	2,700	150,000
Stein	220,000	2,700	150,000
Villenave	220,000	2,700	
Duchesne	240,000		
Hassel	250,000		
Streit	250,000	4,000 to 5,000	
André	250,000	4,000	40,000
Malchus	250,000	4,000	100,000
La *Revue Britannique* (1827)	250,000	4,000	100,000
Bisinger	250,000	4,000	100,000
Amati	260,000	5,000	
Breslau			
University Library			
Stein	100,000		
André	100,000		
Ebert	100,000		
La *Revue Britannique* (1827)	100,000		
Malchus	100,000		
Bailly (1833)*	100,000		
Hassel	115,000		
Zedlitz	130,000 to 140,000		
Allgem. Handl. -Zeitg.	160,000		
Wachler	200,000	2,300	
Goettingen			
University Library			
Amati	200,000		
Ebert	200,000		
Schubert	200,000		
Schnabel	200,000		
Villenave	200,000	5,000	110,000
Streit	240,000		
Stein	240,000		
André	280,000	5,000	110,000
La *Revue Britannique* (1827)	280,000	5,000	110,000
Bailly (1833)†	280,000	5,000	110,000
Hassel	295,000		
Allgem. Handl.-Zeitg.	300,000		
Quarterly Journal of Education (1831)	300,000		
Wachler	300,000		

In the Journal de la Société française de Statistique Universelle.
†*In the* Journal de la Société française de Statistique Universelle.

Authors	Volumes	Number of Manuscripts	Theses, brochures, fugitive items, etc.
Malchus	300,000	5,000	
Conversations-Lexikon	300,000	5,000	
Bisinger	300,000	5,000	
	Wolfenbüttel Ducal Library		
Schubert (1824)	100,000		
La *Revue Britannique* (1827)	109,000	4,000	40,000
Bailly (1833)*	109,000	4,000	40,000
Stein (1827.*Reisen*, etc.)	120,000		
Hassel	190,000		
Stein	190,000		
André	190,000		
Ebert	190,000	4,500	
Villenave	190,000	4,500	40,000
Streit	200,000		
Bisinger	more than 200,000	4,000	100,000
Amati	200,000	10,000	
Malchus	210,000		
Neue geogr. Eph. de Weimar	280,000		
	Freiburg University Library		
Hassel	19,000		
Malchus	30,000		
Ebert	70,000		
Schubert	100,000		
Stein	100,000		
Schreiberg	100,000		
	Stuttgart Royal Library		
Amati	more than 30,000		
Ebert	130,000		
Malchus	144,000	3,000 to 4,000	
Wachler	150,000		
Memminger	from 150,000-200,000		
Plieninger	160,000	1,800	137,000
André	170,000		
Bailly (1833)†	170,000		
La *Revue Britannique* (1827)	170,000		
Villenave	180,000		
Hassel	200,000		
Bisinger	200,000		
Stein	200,000		
Streit§	200,000		

In the Journal de la Société française de Statistique Universelle.
†*In the* Journal de la Société française de Statistique Universelle.
§*Without the manuscripts and incunabula.*

Authors	Volumes	Number of Manuscripts	Theses, brochures, fugitive items, etc.
Munich Royal Library			
The author of *8 days in Munich*	250,000*	16,000	400,000†
Dibdin	300,000§		
Villenave	300,000	9,000	
Ebert	300,000	9,000	
Hassel	400,000		
La *Revue Britannique* (1827)	400,000		
Malchus	400,000		
Bailly (1833)**	400,000		
Amati	more than 400,000		
Hohn	more than 400,000		
Streit	400,000	8,000	
Bisinger	400,000	10,000	
Schnabel	400,000	90,000	
Duchesne	500,000		
D'Haussez	500,000††		
Wachler	600,000		
Copenhagen Royal Library			
Schnabel	130,000	many	
André	130,000	3,000	
Ebert	200,000	many	
Villenave	more than 200,000	10,000	
Amati	250,000		
Hassel	260,000		
Malchus	260,000		
Bisinger	260,000		
Stein	300,000		
La *Revue Britannique* (1827)	300,000 to 400,000	many	
Werlauff	almost 400,000		
L'Hertha	400,000		
Bailly (1833)§§	400,000	many	
Le *Messager du Nord*	500,000		
Les *Berl. Nachr.* of 1825	500,000***a large number		
Les *Eph. de Weim.* in 1825	500,000†††a large number		

*Different works.
†Of which 300,000 small brochures and 100,000 theses.
§In this number are included the duplicates and manuscripts.
**In the Journal de la Société française de Statistique Universelle.
††In this number are included 18,000 manuscripts.
§§In the Journal de la Société française de Statistique Universelle.
***This is the number of printed works.
†††This is the number of printed works.

Authors	Volumes	Number of Manuscripts	Theses, brochures, fugitive items, etc.
Oxford Bodleian Library			
Bisinger	130,000		
Meidinger	130,000	20,000	
Haendel	180,000	17,000?	
The *Quarterly Review* (1826)	more than 200,000		
Ebert	300,000	25,000	
Villenave	300,000	25,000	
Malchus*	400,000		
Bailly (1833)†	400,000	25,000	
La *Revue Britannique* (1827)	400,000	25,000 to 30,000	
Stein	500,000		
Andr	500,000	30,000	
Cannébich	500,000	30,000	
Conversations-Lexikon	500,000	30,000	
Schnabel	700,000	30,000	
Le *Guide d'Oxford*§			
Edinburgh Advocates Library			
Hassel	30,000		
Ebert	50,000		
Malchus	70,000		
La *Revue Britannique* (1827)	about 80,000	1,600	
Bailly (1833)**	80,000	1,600	
Meidinger	100,000		
Haendel in his ref. 1827	120,000		
Chamber	120,000		
Stark	150,000		
M. de Nagy	150,000		
University Library			
Bailly in (1833)††	50,000		
Hassel	50,000		
Malchus	50,000		
Villenave	50,000		
Conversations-Lexikon.	50,000		

*By combining the three Libraries Bodleian, of Radcliffe and of Christ-College.
†In the Journal de la Société française de Statistique Universelle.
§The author of the New Pocket Companion for Oxford, etc., published in that city by Cook in 1802, comments as follows on this library: "That it contains more books than any other library of Europe, except the Vaticana." We relate this remark because it is probably the original source which has induced more than one famous statistician and geographer into error [and] whose opinion has been slavishly adopted by the makers of abstracts and of statistical tables.
**In the Journal de la Société française de Statistique Universelle.
††In the Journal de la Société française de Statistique Universelle.

Authors	Volumes	Number of Manuscripts	Theses, brochures, fugitive items, etc.
La *Revue Britannique* (1827)	50,000	a few	
Ebert	more than 50,000		
Haendel	more than 50,000		
Huot*	more than 50,000		
Meidinger	60,000		
Stark	70,000		
Chamber	70,000		
M. de Nagy	70,000		
	Saint Petersburg Imperial Library		
Bisinger†	from 80,000 to 300,000		
Stein	240,000		
Malchus	300,000§		
Hassel	300,000		
Cannabich	300,000		
André	300,000	11,000	
Schnabel	300,000	11,000	
Le *Bulletin* (1828)**	300,000	12,000	
Stein	300,000	12,000	
Schnitzler	300,000	13,000	

*In the two editions of the Précis of Malte-Brun.
†Citing Hassel for the first estimate, and Galletti for the second.
§Including the library of the Hermitage.
**The Bulletin des Sciences géographiques of Baron de Férussac, citing l'Hésperus.

Rebuffed by this stunning disparity of opinions we have been on the verge of abandoning such a difficult subject; but regretting the considerable time wasted in these studies, we have forced ourselves to proceed with it. We have even tried to work our way back to the source of these so different opinions and we hope to have found it within the causes which we have indicated in the treatise already mentioned.

This part of comparative statistics is still at the point where the population of the countries was in the second half of the last century. We have only approximate data about the best-known libraries; the most divergent opinions are emitted about the riches of all the others. The nationals repeat sometimes without spirit of criticism the exaggerated evaluations coming from the mouth or the pen of an unconscientious librarian, who believes he will enhance the renown of the establishment which was entrusted to his care by exaggerating the number of its volumes; sometimes, they repeat those which have been handed down from father to son, and which are almost always the most erroneous ones. Sometimes, driven by an excessive amount of self-respect, and based on approximate figures, which they themselves have arrived at on erroneous assumptions, they daringly accuse of inaccuracy the conscientious writer, who will emit an opinion contrary to theirs after having examined everything that has been written about this same library by other educated nationals or by travelers of wisdom who have visited it. There are only too many scholars, who, unversed in the various disciplines around which statistics revolve, accustomed to consider as accurate the erroneous estimates of which all the geographies, all the dictionaries, all the encyclopedias, all the statistical tables, and masses of works which pass for classics are replete, do not hesitate to reject as errors different estimates, which obtained through sheer endeavor, or else, average numbers, are the results of long and fastidious research, obtained by a few statisticians or by a few travelers, who are as educated as they are conscientious.

One of the main sources of this perplexing disparity of opinions is without a doubt the way one goes about calculating the literary wealth of the same library. This author counts only the printed books; that one adds to that number the manuscripts; a third one reduces to a certain number of volumes the theses, the brochures and the fugitive items, which are kept there unbound, in cartons, or bound in volumes, and which the first one has excluded in their entirety; a fourth one, using the same procedure, adds a certain number of volumes for the engravings, the maps and the plans, which, forming part of no particular work, could not be included in the printed books; here comes a fifth one, who, considering all the theses, all the brochures and all the fugitive items as volumes, feels compelled to add their numbers to the one of printed books contained in the library, whose number of volumes he thusly exaggerates in an extraordinary fashion; finally, another one yet deducts from the number of volumes all the duplicates, that is to say those already included in the works counted in the mass of printed books. These different manners of tackling the problem—and a few others, which would be too time-consuming to examine here—must not be confused with those we have related above; they are the main sources of the errors spread by travelers and which scholars, worthy of esteem but through negligence or even ignorance of a few geographers, do not hesitate to reproduce in their works.

The wealth of the libraries stands somewhat on a par with the populations of certain large cities of Asia or Africa, whose censuses made today—or the criticism of competent judges—have reduced the millions of inhabitants to a few hundreds of thousands. In the same way the recently prepared catalogues of a few libraries, or else their inspection performed by travelers versed in statistics or they themselves librarians, have made short work of these popular estimates, to these ridiculous exaggerations, which still spoil rightly famous works, by reducing by one-third, half, and even up to nine-tenths the number of volumes agreed upon, God knows why, to assign to them.

Before the revolution, almost everyone in France carried to 300,000 and even to 500,000 volumes for the *Royal Library*. A discriminating bibliographer, the late M. Barbier, had reduced it to 200,000 volumes in the *Annuaire administratif et statistique du département de la Seine* for the year XIII. (1805). But already its present scholarly librarian, M. Van Praet, having counted in 1791, one by one, the volumes then contained in that establishment, had only found 152,868 of them, of which 23,243 in folio, 41,373 in 4° and 88,252 in 8° or of smaller format.

The author of a scholarly article on the *Library of the City of Lyon* has reduced, not too long ago, to 90,000 volumes the 106,000, the 110,000 and the 120,000, which for some time now people did — and still do — take pleasure to grant to it.

We had always heard it said that the *Library of St. Mark* in *Venice* had 150,000 volumes; we thought we were nearing the truth when we evaluated them at 90,000 in 1822 in the *Statistique du Portugal*; but upon our return to Venice that same year, we were assured by its scholarly librarian, Abbot Bettio, that it counted then only 65,000 volumes and 5,000 manuscripts; it is not without surprise that in 1832 yet we see scholarly statisticians assign it a number of volumes greater than twice that amount.

Popular estimates agreed upon 150,000 and even 200,000 volumes for the *private library* of *George III.*, donated by George IV. to the *British Museum*; the screening has just reduced this number to only 65,000.

M. Schubert, professor at the university of Königsberg, who has performed long studies on this subject, and who has visited the principal libraries of Europe as a scholar and as a distinguished statistician, assured us, in 1824, during his trip to Paris, invoking the authority of M. Reuss, the Head Librarian of *Goettingen*, that this superb establishment, rather generally agreed upon to be credited with 300,000 volumes, did not house many more beyond 200,000.

What shall we say of the ridiculous — not to say absurd — exaggerations, which are found in justly famous works, on the number of volumes of the libraries of the *Vatican* in Rome, and the *Bodleian* in Oxford? What shall we think of the science of geography and statistics when relating them to a learned naturalist, who, in volume VIII. of the *Précis* of Malte-Brun, published in 1829, says, at page 611, that "the Bodleian Library, exception made of the one of the Vatican, houses more books than any other of Europe;" and who, in 1832, at page 78 of the IV.th volume of the second edition of that same work, repeats that "the Bodleian Library, exception made for that of the Vatican and for the Royal Library in Paris, houses more books than any other of Europe"?

Already in the year 1822, in our *Essai statistique sur le Royaume de Portugal*, aided by the knowledge of a learned bibliographer, we have made short work of these exaggerations, estimating the first library at only 60,000 printed volumes and at 60,000(?) *manuscripts*, and by granting the three libraries together (*Bodley, Radcliffe* and *Christ-College*), belonging to Oxford University, only 400,000 volumes and 30,000 MS. We had the pleasure to see our last estimate being adopted by M. de Malchus, although this learned statistician, who is always so conscientious in his citations, has forgotten to indicate the source of his information, which is so at variance with all those that had as yet been made on the number of volumes of the famous *Bodleian Library*. The studies which we have undertaken since and the facts we were able to gather have demonstrated that we were not too far off the truth. Despite the imposing name of Ebert, who in 1823 credited it with 300,000 printed volumes and 25,000 MS.; despite the 400,000 printed volumes and the 25,000 to 30,000 MS. which were assigned to it in 1827 by the anonymous author of the learned article on the principal libraries of Europe, reproduced in the *Revue Britannique* of the same year, we persist in granting the *Bodleian Library* only about 200,000 volumes and 25,000 manuscripts. As support for our opinion we invoke the authority of the scholar Haendel, who, in 1827, gave it only 180,000 printed volumes and 17,000 MS., and the *Quarterly Review*, which, in 1826, carried them only to 200,000. We shall add that a distinguished mathematician, M. de Nagy, member of the Philosophical Society of Philadelphia and librarian of Count Karoly, who, as a scholar, has visited all the principal libraries of Southern Germany, of France, of the United Kingdom and of the Anglo-American Confederation, grants it only approximately that number in a note, which he was kind enough to address us on this subject. We feel even compelled to signal a rather remarkable scientific anomaly; that is: after having attentively perused the whole history of the Unversity of Oxford, published in great typographical luxury in 1814, we have not found in either of its two thick in 4° volumes the slightest trace about the number of volumes contained in the principal and most famous of its libraries.

With respect to the *Vatican Library*, we do not blush in acknowledging that, led into error by imposing authorities, we have exaggerated the number of its manuscripts, although the question mark which accompanied our figure was sufficiently signalling our doubts. However, considering that since that time the library of an illustrious man of letters, the recent loss of whom Italy deplores—of Count Leopold Cicognara—has added close to 10,000 volumes to the printed matter of the *Vatican*, we think that the present number could be increased to almost 75,000; and we reduce to approximately 35,000 that of its precious manuscripts. In support of our estimates we invoke three very competent judges: the scholarly author of the *Iter Italicum*, M. Blume, who credits it with only 30,000 printed volumes and 25,000 manuscripts; and the two scholarly librarians Ebert and Valery, of which the former assigns it only 30,000 volumes and 40,000 manuscripts and the latter increases to 80,000 the printed books and reduces to 24,000 the manuscripts. We shall also recall that M. Cadell estimates the latter at 30,000. We ignore all the other estimates concerning the number of volumes of this library because they are only repetitions of figures set forth by these three scholars, either literal ones or somewhat modified ones with the intent of hiding their origin, or yet they are only opinions of such a ridiculous portent that they do not deserve the honor of a refutation.

We must also admit that we were pursuing more than one purpose as we were drawing up the table which holds our attention, and we believe that we are rendering a service to science and simultaneously performing an act of justice by proclaiming them with candor.

First, by offering to the reader so many different opinions on the number of volumes in the same library, we wanted to give him material proof of the long and fastidious research which we had had to undertake to determine the relative wealth of the principal libraries presently in existence, and in so doing to deserve his confidence, not only with respect to everything we have stated above but also to whatever we still had to tell him on this subject.

Then we wanted:

1. To show by the comparison of the most differing opinions how far the lack of criticism or negligence—not to use a more severe expression—of certain authors can waylay them in their estimates.

2. To point the finger at the origin of certain errors, and to signal to the public those sources, sometimes too little known, from which authors, who are more ambitious than learned or conscientious, draw at little cost their vast erudition.

3. To mention the source where these same authors sometimes repair to draw the documents, which they qualify with the word

"official," as well as the so-called kind communications or even official ones, which they claim to have used as a basis for their statistical works.

4. To render their due to a few journals, which are rightly famous, for their contribution to the progress of that part of statistics as of all the other branches of human knowledge. At page xxiii of the Introduction of our *Abrégé de Géographie* we have not shied away from citing the principal journals from which we had borrowed heavily for its drafting. Without repeating here the long list of their names, we shall remind the reader that it is especially in the principal *Revues Anglaises* and in the *Times*, in the *Revue Britannique*, in that of the *Deux-Mondes* and in the *Bibliothèque Universelle de Genève*, in the *Nouvelles Annales des Voyages*, in those which M. *Berghaus* publishes in Berlin, in the *Jahrbücher der Literatur*, in the *Ausland*, in the *Morgenblatt*, in the *Journal des Débats*, in *Le Temps*, in the *Allgemeine Zeitung*, that we have found a mass of facts, which, soon after their publication — and sometimes even several years later — we saw with surprise appear as "new facts, results of long research and of diverse tricky calculations," which had never been made, or else as "official documents of which they were supposed to have been furnished with," documents which never came out of any office to enrich the files of certain statisticians. It is to the chief editors of scientific journals, it is to those literary magistrates that the honorable task of condemning these plagiarisms belongs, plagiarisms which hinder conscientious authors in their works and set back the sciences in the middle of their progress by the publication of a shower of works in which, not taking into account what has been done for the advancement of science, they persist in reproducing as new facts, or even as perfections, errors proven as such by their predecessors in special works which were generally and justly applauded.

5. To pay finally a tribute of praise which the scholarly works on the ancient and modern libraries published by Ebert in *l'Encyclopédie d'Ersch et Gruber*, and that, no less remarkable of M. de *Malchus* which forms one of the most interesting parts of his *Statistiques de l'Europe*, deserve. Indeed, these two tables, despite their considerable lacunae, and their errors even, are nonetheless what exists as most scholarly and as most conscientious about this subject, and whatever else has been published since does not offer any of the warranties necessary to deserve the confidence of the public and of scholars. The considerable additions regarding the libraries of France in the recent works of MM. Bailly and Villenave, published in the *Journal de la Société française de Statistique Universelle*, and in *l'Encyclopédie des gens du Monde*, are quite far from having filled the lacunae and from

having corrected the errors that one can hold against the tables of these two German scholars. But if the time of the publication of the article of the librarian of Dresden lends excuses for its imperfections, one cannot feel equally indulgent toward the *Statistique des bibliothèques anciennes et modernes* published in 1833 and 1834. It is especially in the latter that we have discerned the largest number of borrowings made from Ebert, without citing him, and, what is more, we noted that in 1834 his erroneous evaluation of the volumes contained in the Royal Library of Berlin had been adopted while in the same breath it cited the history of that establishment published by M. Wilken, who is its head librarian, and who gives such a different number for the volumes than Ebert had assigned in 1823!

It is in this same article that we find that the "library of the Escorial is the first of the Peninsula and one of the richest in the world"! We shall observe in favor of Ebert's opinion, who granted it only 17,500 volumes and 4,300 manuscripts, after an exact enumeration made by Ximenes, who published its history, that, not in a position to reasonably revoke, to doubt the positive facts advanced by the latter, the only supposition left open is that since that time this library must have made large acquisitions. But all the information which we have obtained from several Spaniards, whom we had the privilege to be acquainted with, are supporting the estimate of Ebert. Besides, Count de Laborde, who has seen and well described Spain, credits it only with 30,000 volumes in 1820. We are awaiting true official documents or very authenticated facts not only to rank this famous library among the richest in the world but even to assign it the 130,000 volumes that M. André granted it a few years ago, and the 130,000 printed matters and the 15,000 manuscripts granted it by the *Statistics of Spain*, which M. Moreau de Jonnès has just published.*

We were going to hand this paper to the press when, through a stroke of luck we received the February 1835 installment of the Revue Britannique, in which we found an excellent article on that library, [an article] which was made with care and by a scholar who has visited the premises and whose name we regret not to know. We have extracted the following passages, which support what we have elicited and which, in addition to confirming the exactness of Count de Laborde's evaluation, will oblige the reader to brand those estimates as valueless through which authors of our day and age — repeating old errors — attribute 130,000 printed volumes and 15,000 manuscripts [to that library]. "The library of the Escorial," says our anonymous [author], "has three large divisions: the library below, the library above and that of the manuscripts. The first, which is the most considerable one, is composed of three rooms, one of which measuring 190 feet in length and 32 in width. The open cases are magnificent and made out of precious wood. The number of volumes which it contains is approximately 18,000, of which 700 are manuscripts of Greek, Latin or Spanish [works]. Some date from the VII.th and VIII.th centuries.

"The library above contains approximately the same number of volumes as the

It is yet in the article of the *Encyclopédie des gens du monde* that we read with surprise that "the Imperial Library of Vienna is housed in an old church with eight large rooms," and this more than a century after it had been set up in the magnificent building, which Charles VI. had built for that purpose; that in the library of Dresden they preserve "a manuscript written in Mexico," adding that "it is a calendar with a few fragments of the history of the Incas"! But we shall not multiply these examples so that the public will not suspect our harboring views which are totally foreign to those we had when we wrote these lines. We shall only allow ourselves to recall that our *Essai statistique sur les bibliothèques principales de l'Europe*, which M. Ebert could not have known when he was working on his own in the beginning of 1823, and which M. de Malchus has had the tactfulness of citing several times, is the first general work so far published on this subject. We shall add that our table is part of a work announced with praise in the *Journal des Débats* by the first judge of competence at the time, published in French and in France's capital, circumstances which, all of them, render impossible the assumption one would be tempted to formulate by seeing authors describe in 1833 and 1834 the principal libraries of Portugal, while citing in support of their erroneous opinions the works of Murphy and of Link!

In order to facilitate for the reader the usage of our table of the different opinions emitted on the number of volumes contained in a few famous libraries of Europe, we have arranged in the following table, in chronological order of their publication, the works whose authors are mentioned. We have not added the journals because the date of their publication is always indicated after their titles in the preceding table, in which are recorded the results of the handwritten communications that we owe to the kindness of MM. *Schubert* and *Nagy* and whose first ones refer to the year 1824 and the second ones to the year 1833. The estimates which we owe to MM. *Gironi* and *Ferrucci*, head librarians of the libraries of Brera in Milan and of the University of Bologna, also refer to that same time period. The [estimate] of *Umili*, concerning the library of the Borbonica Museum in Naples, refers to the year 1826.

(cont.) first. It was destined to be an annex [to the first], with the same subdivisions.

"*The most important part of the library is that of the manuscripts. The room which houses them is spacious and the open cases are of great beauty. The Arabic manuscripts, if one is to attach any faith to the catalogue, are far from filling the room outright. A large number of Greek and Latin manuscripts have been placed there; but one of the principal objects, which is shown to the curious [visitors] of that room is a Koran written in the middle of the IX.th century, in colored letters, for the use of one of the first kings of Cordova. In addition to the manuscripts carried in the catalogue, and which number 1,631, there are several incomplete ones that were pulled out of a fire.*"

Chronological Table
of the Time of Publication of the Works whose Authors
are Mentioned in the Preceding Table

Years	Names of the Authors and Titles of Their Works
1817	*Eustace*: Voyage classique en Italie.
1819	*Petit-Radel:* Recherches sur les Bibliothèques anciennes et modernes.
1819-1827	*Stein*: Dictionnaire géographique; la 4. édition de sa Géographie; et ses voyages aux principales capitales de l'Europe.
1819-1824	*Hassel:* ses différents ouvrages, publiés pendant ces cinq années sous différents titres.
1820	*Laborde:* le 2 volume *in folio* de son voyage pitoresque en Espagne.
1821	*Dibdin*: Voyage bibliographique et pittoresque dans l'Allemagne et en France.
1821	*Blanchard-Boismarsas*: Itinéraire d'un ami des arts, ou statistique générale des académies et des bibliothèques de Paris et de la France.
1822-1823	*Ebert*: Histoire de la Bibliothèque Royale de Dresde; et son grand article sur les bibliothèques anciennes et modernes dans l'Encyclopédie D'Ersch et Gruber publiée à Leipzig.
1823	*André*: Statistique des chiffres.
1823	*Bisinger*: Tableau comparatif des forces et des ressources de tous les Etats de l'Europe.
1824-1830	*Blume*: Iter Italicum.
1825	*Wurlaff*: Histoire de la Bibliothèque Royale de Copenhague (en Danois).
1826	*Malchus*: Statistique de l'Europe.
1827	*Le Conversations-Lexikon* publié à Leipzig.
1828	*Wilken*: Histoire de la Bibliothèque Royale de Berlin.
1828-1831	*Zedlitz*: Statistique de la Monarchie Prussienne; et son Guide du Voyageur dans la même Monarchie: Berlin.
1828	*Bailly*: Notices historiques sur les bibliothèques anciennes et modernes.
1828	*Amati*: Ricerche storico-critiche-scientifiche sulle origini: Milano.
1828	*Meidinger*: Voyage dans l'Archipel Britannique.
1829	*Schnitzler*: Essai statistique sur l'Empire Russe.
1829	*Galanti*: Napoli e Contorni di Giuseppe Maria Galanti, nuova edizione interamente riformata.

Years	Names of the Authors and Titles of Their Works
1830	*Haendel*: Catalogue des manuscrits contenus dans les biblio-thèques de la Suisse, des Pays-Bas, du Royaume-Uni, de l'Espagne, etc.
1831-1833	*Schnabel*: dans la 7. édition de la géographie de *Galletti*, et dans sa statistique de l'Europe.
1831	*Streit*: dans son Guide du Voyageur de Reichard.
1831	*Stark*: Picture of Edinburgh.
1831-1833	*Valery*: Voyages historiques et littéraires en Italie.
1832	*Cannabich*: Manuel de Géographie.
1832	*Garinei*: libraire éditeur de la *Guida della città di Firenze*.
1832	*Rampoldi*: Corografia dell' Italia.
1833	*Wachler*: Histoire de la littérature.
1833	*Chamber*: Dictionnaire géographique de l'Ecosse.
1833	*Hohn*: Statistique du Roy. de Bavière.
1834	L'auteur anonyme des *Huit jours à Munich*.
1834	*Duchesne*: Voyage d'un Iconophile.
1834	*Plieninger*: Description de la ville de Stuttgart.
1834	*Villenave*: dans l'article *Bibliothèques* de l'Encyclopédie des gens du Monde.
1835	*d'Haussez*: Voyage d'un Exilé.
1835	*Stein*: Description statistique et géographique du royaume de Saxe.

One will perhaps be astonished at not seeing in the above table the names of authors of a mass of geographies, statistical [works] and geographical dictionaries, which are in everyone's hands. The only excuse we shall proffer is that having offered to the reader the names of the authors of the original works, we have thought it practically use-less to lengthen the list by intercalating those of their non-confessed plagiarists and translators.

VIII. Comparison of the Imperial Library with the Largest Libraries of the World, Ancient and Modern

The table that we are going to give offers the largest libraries in the world presently existing. Knowing with relative precision the number of volumes they contained a few years ago, we have attempted to estimate approximately those they contained at the conclusion of the year 1833. We excluded from the list all the libraries that did not count 150,000 volumes regardless of their fame or importance. That is the reason why the reader should not attempt to find any of the libraries *Vatican, Laurentian, Ambrosian* nor those of the *Institute Royal* of *France*, of the *Academy of Sciences* of *Saint Petersburg*, of the *Universities* of *Bologna*, of *Turin*, of *Prague*, of *Leipzig*, of *Glasgow*, of *Dublin*, of *Christiania*, etc., etc.; nor any of those precious libraries which Holland, Belgium, Sweden, Switzerland, as well as several cities of France, of Germany, of Italy, and a few of Spain, of Portugal and of the United States possess. These latter, ordinarily quite outstanding by their selection of books, are very far from being comparable to the libraries of Europe, even to those of fifth rank, with respect to their number of volumes. It could not be otherwise since all these establishments beyond the Atlantic are of too recent an origin to have been able to gather a large number of volumes. We shall state even that we know not a single library of America that contains more than 50,000 volumes. This number, with which in another of our works we had credited the *Imperial Library* of *Rio de Janeiro*, being only approximate, we have even some reasons to believe is more or less exaggerated. We borrow from our work, which is still in the handwritten stage, the following table, which is only a fragment of the statistics of the principal libraries of the New World; it offers the six most considerable libraries of the Union, calculated for the end of the year 1833. A part of it is drawn from the excellent work, which M. Worcester publishes yearly, with another esteemed scholar, under the modest title

of *American Almanac;* we owe the remainder to the friendship of M.
de Nagy, who, as we have stated it elsewhere, has just visited them.

Statistical Table
of the Principal Libraries of the Union

Names of the Cities	Libraries	Number of the Volumes
Philadelphia	*Loganian Library*	42,000
Cambridge	*Harvard University Library*	40,000
Boston	*Athenaeum Library*	26,000
New York	*Athenaeum Library*	25,000
Washington	*Library of Congress*	16,000
Charleston	*(South Carolina) Society Library*	15,000

We will perhaps be countered [with the allegations] that the
Royal Library of Stockholm contains no less that 250,000 printed
volumes and 5,000 manuscripts according to the *Notices Historiques
sur les Bibliothèques anciennes et modernes* published by M. Bailly in
1828, and that this scholarly librarian has just reproduced in the
Journal de la Société française de Statistique Universelle; that M. Huot,
in the 2nd edition of the *Précis de Malte-Brun,* grants to the *Advocates
Library* at Edinburgh only 70,000 volumes, even if he includes those of
the Library of *Notaries* and of a *third one* which he does not identify;
that neither M. Bailly, nor M. Villenave, in their *Statistique des
principales Bibliothèques anciennes et modernes,* while describing the
famous *Ambrosian Library,* even cites the one of *Brera;* that if,
by error, we have been the first one to grant in 1822 — against the
opinions of all the geographers and statisticians — 140,000 volumes to
the latter, and if we have been seconded in that opinion by the scholar
M. de Malchus, it is absurd to carry this number to 170,000 today; that
we are also the first one, who, by an unforgiveable exaggeration, have
carried beyond 430,000 the printed volumes alone that are in the *Royal
Library* of St. Petersburg, when an official document, reproduced in
the journals, evaluated in 1831 at only 273,776 the number of its
printed volumes; that it is ridiculous — not to say absurd — to assign
150,000 volumes to the two *Libraries* of *Tokyo* and of *Miako,* about
which we do not have the slightest bit of information, and to grant
280,000 of them to the *Royal Library* of *Peking,* when the scholarly
research of M. Villenave on that subject has permitted him to discover

only two libraries of approximately 30,000 volumes, and which he considers as the most considerable in the whole of China; that it is seen with astonishment that we pass under silence the large *Libraries* of *Constantinople*, of *Morocco* and of *Fez* and even the *Ethiopian Library*, preserved in the St. Croix monastery located on Mount Amara, in Abyssinia, whose origin tradition pushes back to the Queen of Sheba, a contemporary of Solomon: [a library] to which, not three centuries ago, they granted *ten million-one hundred thousand volumes*, all of them, so it was assured, written on parchment and enclosed in silken etuis.

However strong these objections may be, we are not in the slightest embarassed to answer them, because we have authentic facts and imposing authorities to oppose them.

The *Royal Library* of *Stockholm* numbers barely one-fifth of the printed books which the scholar who heads the library of the City of Paris grants it. Without reducing it to 20,000 volumes which Peignot gave it in his dictionary of Bibliology, or reducing it to the 40,000 granted it by the scholar Ebert in 1823, we shall credit it with 50,000 printed volumes and 3,000 manuscripts, this according to valuable information on several branches of the statistics of the Norwegian-Swedish monarchy, which we owe to the kindness of Count Lowenhielm, ambassador of the King of Sweden to Paris in 1829. It is in these same notes that we find that the Library of the University of Uppsala, which is the richest of the whole kingdom, counted at that same time 80,000 volumes and several thousands of manuscripts. These evaluations are almost identical with those we have received from other very distinguished Swedes, who were kind enough to help us with their knowledge in the drafting of our *Abrégé de Géographie*.

The *Advocates Library* at Edinburgh is the first of Scotland; it is richly endowed and receives a copy of all the publications made in the United Kingdom. These circumstances have induced us to adopt the evaluation of M. Stark, author of the interesting *description picturesque* of that town, published in 1831, [an evaluation] which does not differ much from that of Chamber, which must refer to a few years prior to that date: it is almost identical with the one a very educated and well-informed observer, M. de Nagy, has just furnished us. In the face of such positive facts, the approximate estimates, already obsolete [anyway], of compilers of geographies and of statistical tables do not and cannot carry any weight.

It is neither after the descriptions of Milan made by *tourists* nor after the ones that are found in old travelers' guides, that already in 1822 we were first for granting 140,000 volumes to the *Brera Library*, totally forgotten or barely mentioned in the statistical tables; it was, however, after we ourselves had gathered information during our stay in that capital. Now we carry them at 170,000 after the positive information which its scholarly librarian, Counselor Gironi, has just given us through the intermediary of our esteemed friend, Colonel Vacani, the famous historian of the *Campagnes des Italiens en Espagne.** The untiring zeal and the diversified knowledge of M. Gironi, who for the past several years has headed this magnificent establishment, one of Maria Theresa's creations, have made it the first library of Italy, not only because of its number of volumes but also by their discriminate selection, because M. Gironi, in all his acquisitions, has always decided to buy preferably all the most useful books, and especially those costly works which are above the means of professors and of simple individuals. It is for this, as well as for being perfectly current about the sciences and the arts and for carrying a double catalogue, one by authors, one by subject matter, both perfectly drafted, that we must place it so high, not only among the libraries of Italy but also among the largest establishments of this kind that Europe possesses. We shall recall that if we should desire to add to the Brera Library, the *Library* annexed to the *Cabinet of Medallions*, the one which belongs to the *Academy of Fine Arts* and the one of the *Imperial and Royal Institute of Science*, all [of these libraries] being established

---

*This work, to which the periodical presses of France, Germany and Italy have reserved the highest praise, has brought to M. Vacani diamond rings, gold medals and flattering distinctions on the part of nearly all the sovereigns of Europe. His Majesty the Emperor Francis I., informed by a report of His Excellency Count Kollowrat, Minister of State and of the Conferences, of the difficult situation his publication had brought upon the author, came to his aid with an action of true imperial largesse. Not only did he give him a superb ring of diamonds set with his initials but he also ordered that he be paid immediately the sum of 33,220 francs, the value of all the remaining copies of the edition: in this fashion he liberated in one stroke the scholarly author of the pursuits of his inexorable creditors while at the same time making good his considerable losses brought about by the pirate editions of Florence.

It is with eagerness that we seize this occasion to pay tribute of our gratitude to the memory of the august Monarch who was just been committed to his tomb, and we do so the more willingly on account of what he has done for us and for M. Vacani, demonstrating thereby how much his actions belie those who reproach him for not having done anything for the sciences or for those who cultivate them. Following two reports made by Prince Metternich and by His Excellency Count de Kollowrat about our works and about the dire situation in which we were laboring after twenty-five years of the most assiduous scientific works, honored by the unanimous approval of the scholars and of the public, this Monarch had them pay us the arrears of a pension, to which we could not legitimately lay claim because of our prolonged absence from the Empire of Austria, summoned us to Vienna with the title of Imperial Counselor and, granting us a decent salary and total leisure of our own time, allowed us not only to fulfill our engagements contracted with the booksellers of Paris but also enabled us to execute other important scientific works which we had planned to undertake and which it would have been impossible to perform with the limited means which we could have enjoyed by living in Italy.

in the same building as several parts of the large public library, the latter would not count less than 200,000 volumes; this explains the large difference existing between the evaluation given by M. Gironi and the one of M. Rampoldi, both of which we mentioned at page 36.

If we are the only one to carry so high the number of volumes of the *Imperial Library of St. Petersburg*, this is due to the fact that we have been assured that the large library of Warsaw and a part of that of Prince Czartoryski, formerly existing at Pulawy, had just been added to it. Indeed, if one adds these two masses of books to the 278,252 volumes which this establishment possessed in 1832, according to the extract of the official report of the Ministry of Public Instruction, whose communication we owe to the kindness of M. Klaproth, we should have a sum which would rather be higher than lower than the number we have assigned to it in the table on page 57.

There are in Japan, writes to us the scholarly and conscientious M. Siebold, who returned from there laden with a mass of new facts and of precious collections, in answer to our queries, many rich libraries. They belong to the princes, to the important personalities and to the monasteries. In addition to the printed works of the empire, they contain a large number of ancient and modern Chinese works, and even very rare Japanese and Chinese manuscripts, geographical maps, topographical plans and drawings of the natural sciences. A few amateurs possess even remarkable collections of European works, especially Dutch, concerning anatomy, medicine, travel, natural history, and a host of scientific and language dictionaries. The commerce of book-selling plays an important role in that empire. One can state that at Miako, Tokyo, Osaka and Owari, where exist the largest xylographic establishments, they print yearly close to 5,000 to 8,000 volumes, woodprints, geographical maps, etc. The *Libraries* which are the most famous are that of the *Shogun*, or the civilian Emperor, at *Tokyo*, and that of the *Mikado*, or the ecclesiastical Emperor, at *Miako*. The princes of *Satsuma* and of *Kyushu* possess also large collections of books: the one belonging to the latter contains, among others, a handwritten, modern work on the natural history of the whole empire, so detailed, that the woodprints alone which set it forth form 800 volumes in 8°; they represent an infinity of different objects, are colored and have been executed by the best artists of Japan. Despite the accumulation of such bibliographical riches and the great activity of the press, which tends to increase them every year, the famous traveler, to whom we owe these interesting communications, has not dared to assign even an approximate number of volumes to any of these establishments. While rendering homage to his reserve, which should deserve being emulated by a goodly number of travelers and geographers, who, by daring assertions slice through the most difficult questions, which they are sometimes totally unaware of, we do not hesitate to estimate at close to 150,000 the number of volumes of each of the two *Imperial Libraries* of *Tokyo* and of *Miako*. What we have just stated makes these evaluations extremely probable, and we do not know anything that could reasonably negate them.

We respect the results of the scholarly studies of M. Villenave on the wealth of the principal libraries of China; but we persist in still giving at least 280,000 volumes to the *Imperial Library* of *Peking*; this estimate, which we owe to the famous Orientalist, Abel Remusat, too soon carried off from his friends and the historical sciences, whose boundaries he promised to push back, is recorded in our *Abrégé de Géographie* and has already received the sanction of the first [among] living Sinologists, of M. Klaproth, who has reviewed the full description of Asia contained in that work, in which, in round numbers, it was estimated at 300,000 volumes, the *maximum* of the limits (280,000 and 300,000) fixed by Abel Remusat.

A famous Orientalist, M. de Hammer, whom we always find on the first row when there arises a question about the Ottoman Empire, just recently has summarized all the bibliographical wealth of Constantinople, which has been so strangely exaggerated. In the first edition of his history of that empire, M. de Hammer names the 40 libraries which its capital possesses presently, enumerates their wealth, and observes that most of them count only 2,000 volumes, some 2,500; and that the sum of all their bibliographical riches would not exceed 100,000.

What shall we say about the large *Library* of *Fez*, of that of *Morocco* and of the marvelous *Abyssinian Library*? With respect to the first two, we encourage the reader to read the *Voyage d'Ali-Bey* and, especially, the *Specchio geographicostatistico dell'Impero di Marocco*, which M. *Graeberg de Hemso* has just published, a work in which this famous scholar has made short shrift of all the absurdities that geographers and men of letters still emit about literary treasures, which have been dispersed centuries ago. Despite the great name of Kircher, we shall relegate to the *Contes des Mille et une Nuits* everything that is being said about the *Library of the Convent of St. Croix* and about its ten million one hundred thousand volumes.

For what concerns the two largest libraries of *Alexandria*, of the *Ulpian* in *Rome*, of the *Library of the Kadis*, in *Tripoli* of *Syria* and of those of the *Caliphs* in *Cairo* and in *Cordova*, we suggest that the reader meditate about what we shall say below when we shall talk about the largest libraries of antiquity.

But we cannot speak of these vast collections of manuscripts without involuntarily thinking about the largest mass of written paper that has ever been collected in one sole building. We mean the *Archives générales de Venise*, gathered since a few years ago by order of Emperor Francis I. in what was formerly the convent of the *Frari*, at an expense of almost 500,000 francs. This superb establishment, unique of its kind, is composed of 1,890 different archives, housed in 298 rooms, salons and hallways, and does not count less than 8,664,709 volumes or fascicules, containing about 693,200,000 leaves. If we wanted to reduce them in volumes at 200 leaves apiece, so as to be able to compare them in this material fashion to the largest libraries of the world, we would find that these archives would not have less than 3,466,000 of them!*

Comparative Table
of the Greatest Libraries of the World, Ancient and Modern

Numbers of		Names of	
Cities	Libraries	Volumes	Manuscripts
Paris:	Royal Library	626,000	80,000
Munich:	Royal or Central Library	540,000	16,000
St. Petersburg:	Imperial Library	432,000	15,000?
Copenhagen:	Royal Library	410,000	16,000?
Vienna:	Imperial Library	284,000	16,000
Berlin:	Royal Library	280,000	5,000
Peking:	Imperial Library	280,000	
Dresden:	Royal Library	260,000	2,700
Goettingen:	University Library	250,000	5,000
London:	British Museum Library	220,000	22,000†
Oxford:	Bodleian Library	200,000	25,000
Wolfenbüttel:	Ducal Library	200,000?	4,500
Madrid:	Royal Library	200,000	2,500?
Paris:	Arsenal Library	186,000	5,000
Stuttgart:	Royal Library	174,000	1,800
Milan:	Brera Library	169,000	1,000
Naples:	Library of the Borbonica Museum	165,000	3,000
Florence:	Magliabecchiana Library	150,000	12,000
Breslau:	University Library	150,000	2,300
Munich:	University Library	150,000	2,000?
Edinburgh:	Advocates Library	150,000	6,000
Tokyo:	Library of the Shogun	150,000?	
Miako:	Library of the Mikado	150,000?	
Alexandria:	Greatest of the Ptolemic Libraries	110,000??	

*See Appendix 1 for the statistics of these Archives.
†Not included are the 19,093 charts, certificates and original documents.

Names of		*Numbers of*	
Cities	*Libraries*	*Volumes*	*Manuscripts*
Tripoli of Syria:	Library of the Kadis	110,000?	
Cairo:	Caliphs Library	110,000?	
Alexandria:	The library burned by the Arabs	100,000??	
Rome:	Ulpian Library, founded by Trajan	100,000??	
Cordova:	Caliphs Library, founded by Al-Haken	100,000??	

In meditating on the positive facts offered by the above table, one sees that the *Royal Library* of Paris is not only the largest which exists but even [the largest that has] ever existed; that the one of *Munich* comes immediately thereafter; that the third place is due *St. Petersburg* and the fourth to the one of Copenhagen; that the *Library of Vienna*, which we have seen in first position until 1789, has regressed to fifth position by the extraordinary circumstances, which, since that date, have so powerfully contributed to the speedy increase of the libraries which [now] precede it. It is also singular to see five little states, such as the *Duchy of Brunswick*, the *Kingdom of Saxony*, those of *Würtemberg* and of *Hanover*, and the *Grand Duchy of Tuscany*, emerge in a table by their large libraries, [a table] from which are excluded several of the largest states in the world. We can also rightfully wonder when seeing voluminous geographies, recently published, citing — and even describing — the libraries of *Rudolstadt*, of *Schaffouse*, of *Düsseldorf* and others, when they do not even cite the library of Munich, those of Dresden, of Brera and of Edinburgh!! There would be a host of other remarks and comparisons to be made, which we had better commit to silence; because the simple inspection of this table suggests them to any reader accustomed to reflecting on figures.

IX. The Royal Library in Paris Is the Largest Which Exists and Which Has Ever Existed

The doubts raised by some scholars about the number of volumes we have assigned to the Royal Library in Paris as early as 1822, doubts which have become stronger yet by the considerable increase we have recorded since, demand a justification on our part; we are the more willing to oblige as it gives us the opportunity to detail the method we have used to give some basis of comparison to the different elements that compose the wealth it contains as opposed to the corresponding wealth of the principal libraries of the world.

Thanks to the kindness of the librarians in charge of the printed books, MM. Van Praet and de Mane, we know that in 1822 the *Royal Library* possessed:

> 450,000 volumes;
> 450,000 brochures, pamphlets and fugitive items, theses, etc., bound in volumes, or enclosed in portfolios or boxes;
> 80,000 manuscripts, among which are the printed Chinese books, etc.
> 1,200,000 charts, diplomas, etc.;
> 6,000 volumes and portfolios containing 1,200,000 prints.

We shall recall that the 450,000 volumes and the 450,000 brochures, etc., whose numbers we were first to publish in the *Statistique du Portugal*, have since been adopted by several authors and by several journals without their ever having indicated their source; and, that a famous statistician has even addressed us the reproach of having exaggerated the riches of this library by carrying them to 900,000 volumes, a figure which apparently he had obtained by adding two items as different as are *volumes* and *brochures*, which, as we shall see below, would have given him, after having adjusted for their disparity, but 495,000 volumes instead of the 900,000 which he attributes to that evaluation!

Now, to establish a correspondence between these different elements, we shall suppose:

1. that each manuscript forms a volume; which does not present anything of an extraordinary nature since this is the most common method used by public libraries to enumerate their possessions of manuscripts;

2. that each ten brochures, pamphlets, theses and fugitive items put together form one volume, which is a very moderate way to go about their calculation because an ordinary volume in $8°$ contains only from 16 to 18 leaves;

3. that 50 charts, certificates, etc., put together form a volume.

By operating these reductions, we shall have 450,000 brochures, fugitive items, etc., equivalent to 45,000 volumes; 1,200,000 certificates, charts, etc., equivalent to 24,000 volumes. Considering the manuscripts and the 6,000 volumes and portfolios of prints as as many volumes, we shall have for the grand total of volumes existing in the Royal Library in 1822:

> 450,000 volumes of all kinds of formats,
> 45,000 volumes for the brochures, etc.
> 24,000 volumes for the certificates, charts, etc.
> 80,000 volumes for the manuscripts,
> 6,000 volumes for the engravings, prints, etc.
>
> Total   605,000 volumes.

At the same time MM. Van Praet and de Mane assured us that the Royal Library increased yearly by about 4,000 volumes and 3,000 fugitive pieces, brochures, pamphlets, etc., printed in France, and by about 3,000 volumes acquired in public sales or abroad.

Since 1822 the activity of the press has experienced a great upswing. The following table, which we have drafted by combining the data published by M. Beuchot with those furnished to us by the *Catalogue manuscrit des livres et brochures*, etc., *déposés à la Bibliothèque du Roi*, whose communication we owe to the kindness of M. de Mane, shows its [i.e., the press's] evolution and has given us the means to calculate approximately the growth of this establishment due solely to the productions of the French press. Since we did not receive the manuscript Catalogue of the library until the 3rd quarter of the year 1828 and that since then scientific works of a different order have prevented us from consulting it again, we have thought of completing it by an approximate calculation founded on the proportion existing between the productions of the French press recorded in the *Journal de la Librairie*, edited by M. Beuchot, and the same productions recorded during the corresponding years in the *Catalogue de la Bibliothèque du Roi*. The facts contained in the 2nd and 3rd columns of the table below offer the elements of our calculations and the basis of the inductions that we shall deduce from them.

Table
of Articles Printed in France

| Year | Number of Articles | |
	Recorded in the Journal de la Librairie	Entered in the Catalogue de la Bibliothèque du Roi
First period		
1822	6,893	7,016
1823	7,213	6,900
1824	8,337	7,994
1825	8,971	8,723
1826	9,754	10,655
1827	9,800	16,744
Total of the first period:	50,968	58,032
Second period		
1828	9,022	
1829	9,027	
1830	8,456	
1831	7,390	
1832	7,577	
1833	8,060	
Total of the two periods:	100,500	

We shall say that 50,968 (sum of the works announced by the *Journal de la Librairie* during the 6 years which form the first period) is to 58,032 (sum of the works entered into the *Catalogue de la Bibliothèque du Roi* during those same years) as 100,500 (sum of the works announced in that same *Journal* during the first and second period) is to a number X (sum of the works entered into the *Catalogue* during the two periods added together, or from 1822 through all of 1833). This proportion solved, one finds that X = 114,800.

By estimating with M. de Mane that the number of brochures and fugitive items should be equal to that of the volumes; that the latter form half of the production of the press yearly; and by supposing, as we have just shown it by a more-than-probable calculation, that the sum total of works or articles entered into the Library, from the beginning of 1822 to the 31st of December 1833, was 115,000 in round numbers, we shall have half of that sum, or 57,500, which shall represent the number of volumes, and 57,500, which shall indicate the number of brochures and fugitive pieces. By dividing the latter by ten, we shall have another 5,750 volumes to be added to the first ones.

We have seen previously, at page 60, that the Royal Library, in the beginning of 1822, counted 605,000 volumes. Now, to reach the state of its present holdings, we shall say:

Holdings	existing in 1822	605,000 volumes
Increase	coming from volumes acquired in public sales or abroad	36,000 volumes
Increase	coming from the productions of the French press, setting forth 57,500 volumes for the works and another 5,750 volumes for the brochures, theses, etc., which makes a total of 63,250 volumes, or in round numbers	63,000 volumes
	Total	704,000 volumes

We shall increase the number from 704,000 to 706,000 because the 6,000 volumes, which, in 1822, after an approximate calculation, we were assured, represented the collection of prints, must be carried, today, at more than 8,000, according to the scholarly article published in 1834 by Professor Picot in the *Bibliothèque Universelle de Genève*.

We have just proved that the Royal Library *is the largest which exists*. We shall now prove that it is also *the largest that has ever existed*. Our task is not as difficult as may seem at first.

The number of authors, and, consequently, of books, could not be very large in the golden days of Egypt, Greece and Rome; on the contrary, it must have been very limited because of several reasons which contributed powerfully to delay the production of original works and were a hindrance to the multiplication of their copies. Indeed, the history of cities and of nations and the description of the earth, those two subjects, which have become inexhaustible sources for our authors, must have been quite sterile in those days, when history barely embraced a few centuries and when that part of the earth which was known did not amount to one-sixth of what it is for our geographers and our historians. To these powerful reasons, we must add the scarce and difficult communications which existed between different nations and, for the same state, between its several different cities. In addition, a host of sciences and arts, whose fields have become so vast in our days, were then either unknown or else extremely restricted. This is enough to surmise that, if social circumstances were assumed to be on a par, for every thirty or forty authors that we would count today in a country there must have been barely one or two at that time.

The primary resource used for writing, because of its excessive price or because of its scantiness, created fresh obstacles to the production of new works or to new copies. Besides, the multiplication of the latter being feasible only by the slow and very costly use of copyists, it is nigh impossible to carry the average number of copies of the ordinary work beyond 50 to 60. We shall not stand accused of extraordinarily diminishing the number of copies when one considers that the limits of a *first* edition, as a mean, was only 435, according to M. Petit-Radel. This small number of copies and the barbarous way they waged war must have caused the destruction of a large number of works, raised their price tremendously and rendered more difficult – not to say impossible – their great accumulation in one locale. The difficulty experienced by the bibliomaniacs of our days in gathering certain incunabula and the excessive prices at which we have seen them bought demonstrate how few could survive the short space of four centuries elapsed from their publication to our time. How very few copies of a work composed in the time of Alexander must have existed in the times of Augustus or of Trajan! In the presence of these kinds of facts, let them come and tell us about libraries with from six to seven hundred thousand volumes! When we witness in our times – despite the large number of journals and authors who will refute them – that travelers and esteemed scholars repeat without any spirit of criticism in their accounts and in their works the popular estimates, almost always erroneous and sometimes ridiculously exaggerated, of the prodigious wealth of certain famous libraries, why shall be admit, as demonstrated truths, the evaluations – contradictory and clearly overdone – of the large libraries of *Alexandria*, of *Rome*, of *Cairo*, of *Tripoli* of *Syria*, and of *Cordova*? exaggerations the more facile to concoct then, when their authors had no control whatsoever to fear. After having reflected for a long time on the subject, we do not hesitate to affirm that it appears quite improbable to us – not to say impossible – that a single library in antiquity or in the Middle Ages should ever have succeeded in gathering more than 300,000 to 400,000 volumes.

But even if we were to grant 700,000 volumes to *the largest* of the *libraries of Alexandria*, of which more than half burnt during the

siege sustained by Julius Caesar in that city; if we assigned the same
number to the immense *library of Tripoli** and to that of Cairo; if
admitting even that the *third library of Alexandria*, destroyed by the
Arabs, should have counted 600,000 volumes, and supposing an equal
number in the *Ulpian* opened in *Rome* by Trajan and in the *library*
founded in *Cordova* by the illustrious Al-Hakem, the *Al-Mamon* of the
Occident, we would still be able to prove that their contents would not
even equal a fifth of a library composed of an equal number of printed
volumes.

　　Everyone who has published works knows, without a doubt,
that, no matter how close and well written one intends the ordinary

　　**Here are a few facts, which are as interesting as they are generally unknown
about the immense libraries of Cairo and of Tripoli. We believe it useless to declare to
the reader that we are a long way from subscribing to the exactness of the evaluations
of the Arab authors cited. The reasoning which we held in the main text proves their
ridiculous exaggerations. We have borrowed these facts from the* Mémoires géographiques et historiques sur l'Egypte *and on a few neighboring regions, collected and
extracted from the Coptic, Arabic, etc., manuscripts of the Imperial Library, published by M. Quatremère in Paris, in 1811.*

　　*The library of Cairo, says Ibn-Aby-Tay, was the most considerable which
existed in the whole Muslim Empire, and could pass for one of the marvels of the
world. It contained, among other works, 1,200 copies of the* Chronicle of Tabary *and
an infinity of books copied by hand by the most famous writers. It was said that it
contained one million six hundred thousand volumes. The library of the Caliphs, says
Makrizy, was in the great palace, and counted 40 rooms, which housed a prodigious
number of books about all types of subject materials. It contained 18,000 volumes on
the science of the ancients. Among the books which were withdrawn from it during the
troubles which disturbed the reign of Mostanser, were 2,400 copies of the* Koran, *all of
the greatest beauty, written by the most artful masters, and enriched with gold, silver
and other ornaments.*

　　*Of all the libraries of which mention is made by the Oriental writers, the most
considerable one, says M. Quatremère, is the one that existed in* Tripoli of Syria. *From
the account of Tahia-ben-Aby-Tay, cited by Ibn-Ferat, an academy, which was the
most magnificent in existence in the world, could be seen in that town. It contained
three million volumes, which treated, all of them, theology, the explanation of the*
Koran, *the science of traditions and literatures. There were 50,000 copies of the* Koran
*and 20,000 commentaries on that book. The Kadis of the Ammar Family displayed the
greatest zeal for the prosperity of that academy. They retained a hundred copyists to
whom they had assigned an annual salary; among them there were 30 who never left
that building either in daytime or during the night. In all the provinces they had
bonded agents who were buying for them the best works they could find. Under the
government of that family the whole of Tripoli had become an academy where all the
types of sciences flourished, and where the scholars of all the countries abounded.
When, in the year 503 of the Hegira, Tripoli fell to the Franks, commanded by
Raymond, Count of St. Gilles; a priest, who had entered into the library, was struck
by the quantity of books it contained. The room in which he was was precisely the one
that contained the Korans. Having seized one of the manuscripts, he recognized this
work. He took a second one, then a third one, and so on, until he had twenty, and
always found the same book. Having declared that this building contained exclusively*
Korans, *the Franks set fire to it and reduced it to ashes. Only a small number of copies
escaped, which were dispersed to different countries.*

manuscript to be, it can always be considered at least to be equivalent to half of the corresponding printing, even if the printing characters used are of the *cicero* or *philosophie* type. What would it be if it were printed in *petit-text* and in other characters smaller yet?

We know that the volumes of the ancient libraries were rolls and that these rolls were written upon, ordinarily at least, on one side only. Thus the written surface of one such roll would compare with only half of the written surface of one of our books, of which each page is covered with characters. Consequently a library composed of 100,000 rolls would not contain more than the material of one of the libraries composed of 50,000 manuscripts.

We likewise know that if a work were divided into ten, twenty or thirty books, there were ten, twenty or thirty different rolls. Thus, for example, the *Natural History* of Pliny, which in its *first* edition of Venice, in 1469, forms only one volume in folio, was divided into 37 books, and would have formed as many rolls or volumes.

If it were permitted to make any comparisons between such dissimilar elements, we would say that we could compare all these rolls of the ancient libraries to our installments of journals or to our in 8° fascicules that they publish by subscription. What would the large library of Paris be reduced to if for one moment we were to entertain the idea that its 616,000 volumes in folio, in 4° and in 8°, that it contains were only 616,000 fascicules of from 5 to 8 leaves? Yet, this is the way that we must estimate the literary riches contained in all the largest libraries of antiquity and of the Middle Ages, which contained rolls, and even those of medieval times which had only manuscripts.

After what we have just said, it seems to us that, everything well taken into account — and despite the most imposing authorities one could invoke to contest it — there has never existed a library in antiquity and in the Middle Ages whose number of volumes could be equal by their material content to a library composed of 100,000 to 110,000 printed volumes.

We hope to have sufficiently justified the selection we have made of the establishments admitted in the comparative table of the principal libraries of the world, the number of volumes to which we have reduced the largest libraries of antiquity and of the Middle Ages, the important rank we have assigned to the Imperial Library of Vienna, and the eminent place that we have given to the establishment of that type which decorates the capital of France.

X. Statistics of the Other Public and Private Libraries of Vienna

But it is time that we speak of other public and private libraries, which make their sojourn so interesting for scholars visiting Vienna.

We shall divide them into two classes, to wit:

1. Libraries which are open to the public without any reservation.

2. Private libraries.

Public Libraries

Outside of the *Imperial Library*, Vienna has only one other library that is entirely public: it is the one of the *University*.

University Library. It is especially at the time of the suppression of the convents under Joseph II. that this library received the largest number of its books. Since 1806 it receives a copy of all the works printed in the government of Lower Austria. The disciplines in which it is the richest are medicine, natural history and ancient theology. We shall note that it is the most consulted of all the libraries of Vienna because in the summer the number of those who visit it daily varies from 120 to 150 persons; during wintertime this figure rises sometimes to 200.

Private Libraries

This classification offers a large number. By comparing first between them the facts collected by MM. Böckh, Schmidl, Pezzl, Blumenbach and Tschischka, then [the facts] which we were able to obtain from several scholars whom we had asked, we find that we could consider bringing to 40 the number of these libraries, not taking into account several others which are inferior to them either by the

number of their volumes or by the selection, the rarity and the importance of the works of which they are composed. But before describing
the most important ones of them we must indicate the three categories
among which we intend to classify them. We think then that we could
distinguish between:

1. The private or special libraries belonging to religious corporations, literary societies, establishments of instruction, or public
administrations.

2. The private libraries belonging to the reigning sovereign and
to the members of his august family.

3. The true private libraries. These belong to individuals in all
the well-to-do classes of society.

Among the libraries belonging to the first subdivision we shall
restrict ourselves with a few details to the following:

Library of the Serving Fathers (Serviten). It is the largest of
those belonging to religious corporations. It is rich especially in works
on theology, canon law and history; it possesses also a few hundreds of
incunabula.

Library of the Augustinians (Augustiner). It is one of the best
organized from among those which belong to religious corporations. It
serves especially for the use of the Institute formed a few years ago for
the higher education of the secular priests. In addition to the most
important works of ancient and modern theology, and the best
editions of the Fathers of the Church, it possesses several rare
manuscripts and several incunabula.

Library of the Abbey of the Scottish Benedictines (Schotten). Its
books are rather well selected for the studies of those who must use
them. It is theology and history which offer the largest number.

Library of Military Archives (Kriegs-Archiv). It forms one of
the three divisions of the magnificent and useful establishment created
in 1801 by the deceased Emperor, after the plan laid out by His Imperial
Highness Archduke Charles, with the purpose of collecting, coordinating and preserving in one building everything that concerns military
subjects, in order to facilitate the research of those who must write the
history of past campaigns, make the plans for those that they might be
called upon to wage, and to conserve everything most remarkable that
military art offers.

The *Library* which forms the first division is very well selected.
Despite its recent origin, it does not count less than 6,626 works on all
the branches of military art and of the sciences which depend on it,
such as mathematics, geography, statistics, history, voyages, etc. In
addition it possesses a beautiful collection of journals and a catalogue
drafted scientifically in 20 large volumes in folio. Its directorship is

entrusted to a hard-working scholar, to Major Schels, rightly renowned for several works and among others for the publication of *l'Histoire politique et militaire de l'Empire d'Autriche* in 10 volumes, and for the edition of the *Journal Militaire Autrichien (österreichische militärische Zeitschrift)*.

The second division is intended for the *printed and manuscript maps*. The former amount to several thousands and form close to 3,000 different works, without counting 73 atlases.*

The third division contains only *manuscripts* and *acts relative to campaigns*, among which we find precious documents, among others manuscripts of the famous Captains Montecuccoli and Prince Eugene of Savoy.

Library of the Theresian Academy (Teresianische). History, geography, natural history and classical literature are the richest disciplines. It counts almost 700 incunabula of which a few are ranked among the rarest. But modern works are in small numbers.

Library of the Polytechnic Institute. It forms one of the principal collections which enrich this magnificent establishment founded in 1815 by the deceased Emperor with the purpose of facilitating progress and the perfection of commerce, of industry and of the art of civil engineering. Although it counts only a few years of existence, it possesses already 3,410 works, all well selected and offering whatever was important in European publications in the main languages concerning physics, chemistry, pure mathematics as well as applied, mechanics, architecture, technology in all its branches, knowledge of merchandise and the science of commerce. It possesses also the main

---

We cannot mention this rich collection without involuntarily thinking about the two Topographical Bureaus of the General Staff directed by the able and scholarly Lieutenant General Count Rothkirch, one existing in Vienna, the other in Milan. The maps, which come from their workshops [drafting rooms], rival, by the correctness of their details, by the beauty of their drawing, and by the finish of their engraving, anything that France and England have produced that is superior in this kind of work. It is with a perfect liaison between the trigonometric networks of all the surrounding countries that the immense work of the survey largely proceeds, that it extends successively on all the countries of the Austrian Monarchy, and that they publish on a large scale reductions based on the new methods. The public is already in possession of the superb maps of Austria, of the Tyrol, of Styria, while the large atlas of the Adriatic Sea and the magnificent map of Lombardy, recently published in Milan, under the direction of General Campana, are considered by the habitues of that art as true models of topographical engraving. Very competent judges have already highly proclaimed the merits of the Topographical Bureaus of Vienna and of Milan, among others the Bibliothèque Universelle de Genève and the Mémorial du Dépôt de la Guerre. The judgment of the latter has therefore more weight because it is a precious miscellany edited for the past few years by the elite of French Geographers, in which the most proper precepts and methods to direct operations of campaign officers and the result of the great operations effectuated are consigned.

journals published on the sciences and the arts taught in the establishment. In 1834 it counted 106 of them, of which 60 were in German, 20 in French, 20 in English and 6 in Italian. The scholar, M. Prechtl, who heads this establishment, whose organization he directed, is also the principal editor of the famous journal published under the title of *Annales de l'Institut Polytechnique* and author of *l'Encyclopédie Technologique*, which is published in Stuttgart.

Library of the Josephine Academy. Although small in numbers, it is remarkable for the choice of its works, which offers the principal publications relative to medicine, surgery, anatomy, botany and natural history.

Library of the Academy of Oriental Languages. Despite the small number of its volumes, it is one of the most remarkable for its speciality and for the time of its founding, which goes back to the year 1754, when Maria Theresa created this institute destined to form twelve young men in the knowledge of languages of the Orient and even to learn most of those spoken in Europe. The names of Thugut, Revizky and Jenisch shine with honor among those of its students. The library contains 800 volumes belonging to Oriental works, 2,000 volumes in different languages, 442 original manuscripts, 103 copies and 15,000 documents, letters, *divani*, etc.

Library of the I.R. Society of Agriculture. It is also a precious and well selected collection, despite the small volume of its volumes. It counts 1,600 different works, of which 590 are essays or theses and 60 journals. It forms part of the interesting collections belonging to this union of zealous patriots who have contributed so much to the perfecting and the progress of agriculture and of cattle raising in the Austrian Empire, especially in the countries included in the Germanic Confederation.

Library of the Observatory annexed to the University. Although founded in 1753 by Maria Theresa this establishment can be considered as a creation of the deceased Emperor because of its new buildings and the purchase of new instruments ordered in 1825 by this Monarch, an impassioned amateur and a practitioner of that science. The annual endowment assigned to this establishment and the grants have permitted M. Littrow, the famous astronomer who is its director, to increase tenfold the insignificant number of volumes which formed the library gathered by his predecessor.

Library of the Philharmonic Society of the Austrian Empire (Gesellschaft der Musikfreunde). Founded in 1814, it possesses already 1,551 works, among which a *facsimile* of the antiphonary of Pope Gregory the Great must be mentioned, the original of which reposes in the library of St. Gall, and which goes back to the year 780; also, the

Tincter: Terminorum musice deffinitorium, considered by Ferkel as the first musical work to have been printed and whose printing was put at the year 1474 by Burney. A large part of the works of this library comes from the legacy made to it by His Imperial Highness Archduke Cardinal Rudolph, who died in 1831. We can also see a collection of 42 volumes in 4° containing the copy of several important passages relative to music, dispersed in a large number of works, very voluminous and of a great price; it has been edited by the secretary of the Society, M. de Sonnleithner. The scores of music, numbering more than 8,000, form a considerable part of the holdings of the library, which in this respect must be considered as one of the rarest that exists. The beautiful collection of painted or engraved portraits of the principal artists or composers and of the instruments are also some of its related possessions.

Library of the Cabinet of Natural History (Naturaliencabinet). It was founded in 1796 with the zoological and botanical Cabinet, to which it belongs. The works of which it is the holder treat only natural history and the sciences which refer to it. All the manuals, all the systems of classification and all the principal works published on that branch of human endeavor can be found next to the most important voyages and the most famous journals which refer to those sciences. The library is intended for the use of the professors and the employees of this beautiful establishment; it counts already 4,200 works.

Library of the Numismatic Cabinet. It forms part of the beautiful Cabinet of the Medals and the Antiques (Münz- und Antikencabinet). It consists of 2,400 works and 2,200 theses distributed in over 120 boxes. Its well selected books treat only history, antiquities, archaeology and numismatics of all the time periods and of all the nations. The alphabetical catalogue by authors and the one by subject material very well prepared by M. Bergmann, one of the librarians, facilitate the use of that library, where the manuscript of *doctrina nummorum veterum* of the famous Eckhel, the Linnaeus of numismatics, is preserved.

Library of the Aulic Chamber (Hofkammer). This beautiful collection of books, all very well selected, is destined to the use of the employees. There are found the best works of geography, of statistics, of political economy and the most important of what has been published on the disciplines concerning administration.

Library of the Imperial Archives. It is controlled by the Ministry of Foreign Affairs and forms part of the Imperial Archives. The latter fill several rooms and contain a host of precious documents, of which several are very old. Among others the collection of all the peace treaties which concern the countries included in the Austrian Empire can be found there as well as the most important diplomatic part of the great, original historical work of Marin Sanudo, in 56 volumes in folio, work which was not known by Daru when he wrote the history of that famous republic. The library per se is rather small but its holdings are well selected for the purpose for which its creation was intended; it comprises especially books on diplomacy, history and diplomatic sciences. It serves for the use of the employees of the Archives and of the outsiders who are authorized to work there.

Here are the principal libraries belonging to the second division:

The Private Library of the Late Emperor Francis I. It is perhaps the most beautiful and best selected library of all the private libraries of the reigning sovereigns of Europe. It is the Emperor himself who started it in his youth, gathering in it all the most remarkable offerings of literature and of the sciences of which he knew several. He devoted particular care to its increase, and during his long and memorable reign spent annually very large sums from his patrimony for the purchase of the works it contains, purchases almost always ordered by himself. It occupies a building of two floors, contiguous to the one that the monarch was residing in. It is composed of three rather spacious rooms and of a cabinet [office], wherein beautiful open cases are arranged in good order all the printed books and the manuscripts. The upper story consists of two large rooms and of a cabinet: it is designed for the collection of prints and geographical maps.

The library does not count less than 29,589 books, outside of several thousands of theses, brochures and other little books. The bindings are generally magnificent and of the greatest elegance; almost all of them were executed by the best artists of Vienna. In this latter respect we must mention the magnificent work presented to His Majesty in 1818, on the occasion of his last marriage, under the title: *Omaggio delle Provincie Venete*; it is a folio volume, a true master-piece in its genre.

Philology, classical literature, voyages, history, geography and, especially, botany, zoology and the imitative arts shine by the number and the choice of their representative works. The books on juris-prudence and those concerning the history of Germany have received a large increase by the merging of the library of the Aulic Counselor, Baron de Frank, which His Majesty bought from the widow of this scholarly magistrate, who died in 1818.

Among the rare and luxury editions, in which this library is so rich, we must mention 714 incunabula, two copies of the great work on Egypt, a copy of the magnificent work on the *Antiquities of Mexico*, published by Lord Kingsborough, the *Magna Carta* printed in golden letters in London in 1816, and a Chinese work in 12 volumes in folio, representing with the greatest of precision the customs, the clothing, the trades and the exercises of the Chinese.

The collection of prints and drawings by hand is composed of 776 portfolios, of which 646 contain close to 70,000 portraits. It is the best selected and perhaps the largest that exists in this genre. We must add to this 22,065 other leaves preserved in 887 large and small containers: they are the greater part of the portraits that were used by Lavater to compose his work on human physiognomies; several of them feature in the margin remarks traced by the hand of that famous author.

The collection of geographical maps and of plans mounted on linen, is composed of 3,400 items, not counting the 108 bound atlases. There is also a copy of all the maps of that part which was surveyed by the registry of the Austrian Empire; this superb copy consists of several thousand notebooks.

Very detailed and very well made catalogues, especially the one of the printed books and manuscripts, drafted by Young, the next to last librarian, facilitate research of all types. M. Kloyber, distinguished scholar, who followed him as librarian, plans to continue this beautiful work of his predecessor, which remained unfinished. Three employees are attached to this library, of whom two are for the books, the geographical maps and the portraits, the third for the prints and the manual drawings. No one is allowed in it without having obtained the special permission of His Majesty the Emperor.

Library of His Majesty the Young King of Hungary, today His Majesty Emperor Ferdinand I. The small library of the late Empress Marie Louise forms its background. A true witness of the tastes of this monarch during his youth, it offers the best works lately published on classical literature, the natural sciences, history, geography and, especially, technology. We shall observe even that the magnificent collection of the manufactured articles of all the branches of industry practiced in the Austrian Empire, that this Prince was able to form in a few years, and which does not count less than 38,000 items, can be considered as the practical part of the technological work contained in his library. It is unquestionably the most beautiful and the most complete collection that has ever been gathered in this genre.* The library possesses already almost 6,000 works, in addition to several thousand engraved or lithographed prints.

Library of His Imperial Highness the Archduke Charles. We can say that it offers only books of perfect choice and the most beautiful editions, either in large or in small format. We find there all the master-

---

See Appendix 5, where we have given the statistics of it.

pieces of the classical literature of all the nations and all the most remarkable works published on history, geography, travel, political economy, agriculture, natural history, antiquities, the imitative arts, and, as we can well expect on the part of a famous captain who is simultaneously one of the more outstanding authors on [military] strategy,* a perfectly well chosen collection of all the books which treat of military art. M. Sengel, esteemed scholar, heading the preservation of these literary treasures, putting to use the advantage of his position, has been working for a few years on an interesting history of the fine arts, therefore consulting the superb collections of this magnificent establishment.

One of the most beautiful collections of prints and of original drawings that exist and a rich collection of geographical maps can be considered as two magnificent accessories of this library. The first was formed by Duke Albert of Saxe-Teschen by spending enormous sums of money; it continues to be considerably enriched, as well as the two others, by sizeable purchases made yearly by their august possessor with as much taste as with deep knowledge.

The collection of engravings is composed of more than 160,000 items. They begin at the cradle of the art, toward the middle of the XV.th century, and come up to our days. We can admire there a large number of the rarest prints, and among the latter several of those which belong to the oldest German and Italian artists, the works of all the great engravers drawn with care and remarkable sharpness as well as a collection of chiaroscuro (mezzotint) as ample as well chosen.

The collection of original manual drawings is perhaps the most considerable one that exists; it is composed of almost 15,000 leaves. The large number of drawings, either completed or only with outlines, of the most celebrated painters of all the schools, offer the means of studying the painting qualities which form their distinctive character.

The collection of geographical maps comprises almost 6,000 leaves, among which one can find what that part of geography can offer as most important and most remarkable, as well as a large number of plans of military operations.

Library of His Imperial Highness the Archduke Jean. To give the reader a real feeling of intimacy for this library, it would require the

Here are the titles of the two most remarkable works, which have found the most flattering reception on the part of people who pursue these difficult subjects. The first has already been translated in French by General Jomini and in Spanish by M. Ramonet; an Italian translation has also made its appearance in Naples, and we learn that another one in English is also in the process of being published. I. Grundsätze der Strategie, erläutert durch die Darstellung des Feldzuges von 1796 in Teutschland. Wien 1813. II. Geschichte des Feldzuges von 1799 in Teutschland und in der Schweiz, vom Verfasser der Grundsätze der Strategie. Wien 1819.

description of everything that is most remarkable, which the *Library of Johann* of Gratz possesses, because this Prince, who has done so much for the development of the industry and the civilization of Styria, which has become his regular residence these last few years, has presented it as a gift in 1826 to that institute which he founded in its capital and which the states of that province have so richly endowed. It consisted of 8,000 volumes, composed exclusively of the main works on the sciences which this Prince cultivated with as much zeal as success; this means that one could find anything that is very important about military art, history, geography, travel and all the branches of the natural sciences. We shall pass under silence his precious collections of mineralogy, of botany and of machinery, because they are foreign to the subject we are treating. But we shall add that the passion of this Prince for the natural sciences, for chemistry and for technology have already incited him to create a new library of about two thousand volumes at *Vordernberg*, a large village of Styria, where His Imperial Highness possesses iron mines and factories, and where he spends a large part of the year.

Library of His Imperial Highness the Late Archduke Antoine. It is the largest private collection ever made especially where the history and geography of Austria are concerned; it counts also several important manuscripts and the most beautiful works ever published on botany, a science which this Prince, who just passed away, practised with a passion, and to the progress of which he has powerfully contributed in the Empire of Austria, in company of their Imperial Highnesses the Archdukes Reinier and Jean.

Library of His Imperial Highness the Archduke Reinier. This library is in Milan in the palace in which the viceroy makes his home. There are especially books of geography, history, travel and the natural sciences, especially botany, which are in the larger number because of the predilection of the august possessor for these interesting disciplines of human knowledge.

Here we are with the private libraries in the true sense of the words. The scope of our work did not permit us to describe them all, so we shall restrict ourselves to give a brief outline on the twelve following ones, which our research — and that of the scholars who were kind enough to help us with their advice — authorizes us to consider as the most important ones in different respects.

Library of Prince Metternich. In 1816, His Majestic Highness Prince Metternich ordered a reading made of the library of the former Abbey of Ochsenhausen, in Swabia, of which his father had become the owner through the stipulations of the Conventions of the Empire in 1803. Eight thousand volumes coming from that library, joined to the many books which served his own use and to the remains of the old library which the Metternich Family had set up in its residence in Koblenz, formed the first nucleus of this library, which this famous statesman established in his magnificent home. Since then the Prince has not neglected a single opportunity to enrich it either by the considerable purchases of rare books in public sales or by the acquisition of whatever most important modern literature has produced. The library counts presently in excess of 22,000 bound volumes and almost 6,000 fugitive pieces. It distinguishes itself as much by the choice of the books as by the beauty of the copies and the elegance of the bindings. It embraces all the branches of knowledge; but, as one should expect it, the dominant taste of its illustrious owner contributed to enrich especially those parts relative to the historical and political sciences, to philology, to natural history, to the fine arts and to the antiquities. Among its bibliographical and literary rarities we must mention 400 volumes of incunabula and 75 manuscripts, of which a few are on vellum and ornamented with elegant miniatures. The cabinet where this Prince works forms part of this library whose open cases are in mahogany worked to perfection.

To complete the identification of the literary treasures possessed by Prince Metternich we should mention the beautiful collection of books on numismatics, which is housed in his castle at *Königswarth*, in Bohemia. It forms part of the nice collection of medals that is preserved there.

Library of the Prince of Liechtenstein. It distinguishes itself as much by the beauty of the edifice as by the quantity of its books. The most numerous works are those on philology, classical literature, history, military art and the fine arts. Several are outstanding by the beauty of their editions.

Library of Prince Esterhazy. Started by Prince Nicolas in 1791, when he gathered all the books of his ancestors and of his brother, books which were dispersed in the different castles of his family, it has been so much enlarged, in so few years, by considerable purchases made since, that already in 1822 M. Böckh estimated the number of its volumes to have reached 20,000. Natural history, travel, philology and the antiquities are the disciplines which are represented by the larger number of works. The magnificent *collection of prints* contained in about five hundred portfolios, placed flat in some three rooms, full of open cases built high enough as to allow leaning on them, can be considered as an appendage of this library; M. Duchesne, the Elder, awards it the third rank among the collections of this type in Vienna.

Library of the Prince of Dietrichstein. It is especially during the last thirty years that its scholarly and witty owner has taken pleasure in enriching it. The historical works, those of geography, of voyages, as well as the memoirs relative to history of today's era are the divisions in which it is best furnished. It shall soon be placed in the beautiful room, which the Prince had built expressly in the new palace which is being built in one of the suburbs.

Library of Prince Razoumoffsky. The principal part is housed in a room remarkable by its beauty and its elegance. The most beautiful works of botany, the most important voyages, the English and French classics form the principal part of this library which its scholarly owner increases daily with the most important publications available in France, in Russia, in Germany and in England. One can also find a collection of geographical maps and of prints, as well as several drawings and plans.

Library of the Count of Schönborn. It is a well selected collection of books, especially rich in voyages, political economy and history. There are also a few precious incunabula and manuscripts.

Library of Count Fuchs. Among the most remarkable holdings of this library we shall restrict ourselves to point out the collection of works of music because of its richness, and the collection of all the funerary monuments of the city of Vienna and of its surroundings, engraved and painted by national artists and brought together in a work published a few years ago by the Count, at his own expense.

Library of the Count of Harrach. It is one of the most remarkable by its choice of books. A magnificent collection of prints forms a part of it.

Library of the Baron of Bretfeld-Chlumczansky. In the last few years it has been increased a great deal by the addition of the one which the late father of the Baron had formed in Prague. It is especially in numismatics and in history that it is richest. The collection of documents relative to the conclusions of the Diets (Landtagsschlusse) of Bohemia, the one of the historical works on that country and the superb collection of numismatic works are the most remarkable part of that library, in which several other collections which we shall not name, being foreign to our treated subject, can be found.

Library of the Knight of Kesaer. Despite the small number of its volumes, we shall not hesitate to rank it among the most remarkable by the choice of its books, by the beauty of its editions, their perfect state of preservation and their beautiful bindings. The most important part consists in the beautiful collection of original editions of the poets and prose writers of Germany from the XI.th century, epoch of the minnesinger until Martin Opiz, restorer of German poetry in the XVII.th century; by including other German works which refer to it and books written in the Gothic language, Anglo-Saxon and Icelandic, it counts not less than 640 works. The other richest disciplines represented are philology, history, and the fine arts.

Library of M. De Hammer. This library, about which all the best guides to the City of Vienna remain silent, is nonetheless one of the most remarkable by its number, and especially the choice, of its books. It is possibly the most complete collection ever gathered on handwritten and printed works relative to the countries which form the Ottoman Empire. It has served its famous owner in presenting the facts of Ottoman history in a new light, which he is ready to publish. Despite the transfer to the Imperial Library that he has made of his historical manuscripts on the Ottoman Empire, M. de Hammer still possesses three hundred of them in other branches of Oriental literature. We shall add that this renowned Orientalist has recently gathered another library almost as numerous as the former one; it is located in Styria in the castle of Hainfeld, which the Countess of Purgstall, born Cranstoun, a famous British family, has just bequeathed to him.

Library of M. Postolaka. Despite the small number of its volumes, it deserves a distinguished place among the private libraries of Vienna, because of its speciality, the choice of its editions, their perfect preservation and the beauty of their bindings. M. Postolaka, who has prepared their catalogue in Greek, enriched with scholarly philological and bibliographical annotations, has restricted himself to the collection of all the Greek authors or translators, ancient and modern, spiritual and secular, who enjoy a certain measure of fame. There are also a few works in foreign languages relative to Greek literature.

We shall not mention the rich *library* of the *Count of Fries* nor that of *Baron Stefaneo*, because after the deaths of their owners they have been dispersed. But we shall say a few words on the two collections that we could not pass under silence because of their importance; they are:

The Historical Collection of M. Kaltenbaeck. It is composed of about 4,000 printed documents relative to the history of Austria. Its scholarly owner is the editor of a rightfully esteemed journal published under the title *Historische Zeitschrift*.

The Drama Collection of M. Castelli. It is one of the most considerable of the Empire. It is composed of more than 10,000 German plays in print, of which several are translations, of about 500 manuscripts, of a collection of more than 400 portraits of actors and actresses and of 300 authors of theatrical compositions of all the nations; finally, of a collection of theatrical announcements since the year 1600. We shall recall that M. Castelli is a dramatic author of esteem and reputed also by his poetry in Austrian dialect.

We believe we would be guilty of an unforgiveable omission in our identification of the principal private libraries of Vienna if we did not speak of a few, which in truth are not located there, but which, belonging to persons whose regular residence is in the capital, seem to us to deserve mention in the statistics which we are outlining. Here are the main libraries which we classify in this category.

The Library of the Count of Kolowrat (Minister of State and of the Conferences). We can consider it as a creation of its famous owner considering the size of his contribution to it. The history, voyages, classical literature, political economy and the sciences which have most to do with them are the branches which count the largest number of works. It occupies six rooms of the Castle of Reichenau in the circle of Königingratz in Bohemia, a kingdom whose rapid progress, made these last years by the population and agriculture as well as by the extraordinary development that industry, commerce and civilization have achieved, is in a large measure the result of the wise and long administration of this noble lord while he was the *great-burgrave* (General Civil Governor), and that of the skillful administrator, Count de Chotek, who succeeded him and who follows his example.

The Library of the House of the Princes of Lobkowitz, today in possession of Prince Ferdinand, head of this family. It is the largest of all the private libraries that we know.* It fills five large rooms of the Castle of Raudnitz in Bohemia in the circle of Rakonitz, and its founding goes back toward the end of the XV.th century. Bohuslaw de Lobkowitz, known by several writings and by his voyages to Greece and the Orient, was its founder. It embraces all the disciplines of human knowledge; history and classical Greek and Latin literatures offer the largest number of volumes. There is a manuscript on parchment containing the masterpieces of Plato to be found there; it is considered as the most complete of all the known ones; Bohuslaw made its acquisition during his voyages in the Orient for the sum of 2,000 ducats, corresponding today to more than 10,000 of them! This library is also remarkable for a large number of incunabula of the most famous typographic centers of the XV.th century. Several are still in *albis*, that is not cut, as the autographed catalogues of Bohuslaw that are kept there prove.

The 300,000 volumes, gathered in Paris by M. Boulard, have been turned over to commerce and to the devotees some time after his death. Besides, it was rather a depot than a library. We are signaling it to the bibliographers as the most considerable ever gathered by an individual without any mercantile purpose. A rather good number of the works existed in several copies; they were ordinarily bibliographic rarities. We know also that charity contributed as much as good taste to the acquisition of this enormous mass of volumes.

The Library of Prince August of Lobkovitz, President of the Aulic Chamber of Mines and of Mints. It is in Prague in the Lobkovitz mansion; the collection of famous Count Slawata, minister of Emperor Ferdinand II. forms its nucleus; it was gradually increased by the acquisition of the beautiful libraries of Count Czernin, of the attorney Putzlacher and a large part of the one belonging to Count Francis de Sternberg.* Its present, noble owner deeply versed in several disciplines and especially in the natural sciences and in history, continues to increase it by new purchases. Rich in every genre, it distinguishes itself particularly by its collection of all the works relative to the history of Bohemia in the proper restricted sense and of the countries which formerly were subordinate to it. Also found there is the *Codex epistolaris* of the collection of the minutes of the autographed letters of King Georges Podiebrad, the most complete collection of the acts of the Diets of Bohemia printed as well as handwritten and almost all the works published in Bohemia or written by national authors.

The Library of the Count of Clam-Martinitz, general aide-de-camp of His Majesty the reigning Emperor. It is in Prague in the palace of this lord. It embraces almost all the disciplines of knowledge and possesses whatever best that has been published in each. Outside of a large number of precious incunabula, it is especially rich in works on the history of Bohemia, of classical literature and on public rights. Among its manuscripts there are ten of the greatest interest: they treat of the Thirty Years War and of the Revolt of Bohemia.

The Library of the Count of Klebelsberg, retired Minister of Finance. It is in Prague in his mansion. It distinguishes itself particularly for its beautiful incunabula and for numerous works on the fine arts.

The Library of the Prince of Kinsky, Counselor to the Chancellery of the Court. It is in Prague; it is especially rich in incunabula, books on natural history, travels and fine arts.

The Library of the Prince of Dietrichstein. It is housed in Nikolsburg in Moravia, in the palace of that Prince, who is also the owner of the one [library] in Vienna. Its founding goes back to the XVII.th century. The most numerous works are those which treat of theology and philology; it suffered great losses during the Thirty Years War.

The Library of the Prince of Schwarzenberg. After having been for a long time in Vienna, it was just transported almost in its entirety

*We shall recall about the latter that the other part has been bought by Count de Klebelsberg, and that the precious library of an illustrious naturalist, of Count Gaspar de Sternberg, brother of the latter, has been given by him, as well as his rich collections of natural history, to the Museum of Prague, of which he is the president.

to Krumau in Bohemia. Its richest disciplines are the Greek and Latin classical literatures and modern literature, German law, civil and canon law, the history of the countries included in the Austrian Empire, natural history, voyages and political economy.

The Library of the Count of Salm. The most numerous works are those which treat of chemistry, of physics, of political economy and of agronomy, sciences which its owner possesses, who is so rightly renowned by his philanthropic efforts for the progress of agriculture and of industry in the German regions of Austria. It occupies a part of the Castle of Raitz in Moravia in the circle of Brunn, not far from the forges and the factories that the Count has established in Blansko.

The Library of Count Louis of Karoly. Perfectly selected and composed of whatever interesting that was published lately in the sciences and in the French, English and German literatures, this library, which increases rapidly by the considerable sums which its owner commits to it, counts already 6,800 works. The most numerous are those which treat of history, of geography and of voyages. A small collection of prints, very well chosen, forms part of it. It is placed in the Castle of the Count at Toth-Megyer, a large village in the neighborhood of Neutra, in Hungary. We shall add that M. Count George Karoly, brother of Count Louis, possesses also a small library, composed of chosen books in the principal literatures of Europe, a part of the world which he has crisscrossed, as well as a few regions of Asia and Africa.

We shall not classify in this category the rich libraries of Counts Teleky, Ossolinsky and Appony, although the Guides to Vienna recently published describe them yet as existing in that capital, but since a few years ago they have definitely been established in other cities. Indeed, the first one is at *Maros-Vasarhely*, in Transylvania, where its proprietor has opened it to the public; the second one has been bequeathed by Count Ossolinsky to the City of *Lemberg*, with a beautiful building and a rich endowment for its upkeep; the one of Count Appony, who has been residing for several years in Paris as ambassador of Austria, has also been housed for a long time already in *Presbourg* in a beautiful building, which this noble lord has built for the convenience of the public and of the studious people who want to frequent it.

We are not going to offer the statistical table of all the libraries of Vienna on which we have given some information. Our estimates are not taken haphazardly in the Guides printed in this city but they are the result of long research and of communications to which we owe the kindness of MM. *Veit, Schels, Bergmann, Kloyber, Sengel, Kensaer, Gros, Strauss* and *Nagy*, who head the libraries of the *Univer-*

sity, of the *Military Archives*, of the *Numismatic Cabinet*, of the *private library* of the late Emperor Francis I., of those of the *Archduke Charles*, of *Prince Metternich*, of *Prince Rasoumoffsky*, of the *Count of Schönborn*, and of the *Count of Karoly*. We owe appreciation to several others, to MM. *Prechtl*, director of the Polytechnic Institute, *Antoine de Kraus*, Aulic Counselor, the Knight of *Kees*, librarian and director of the technological collection of the young King of Hungary and author of several works, *Bartsch*, a scholarly geologist, author of several interesting theses and librarian at the Cabinet of Natural History, *Littrow*, professor of astronomy and director of the Observatory of the University, *Salzbruckner*, very distinguished naturalist and private secretary of Archduke Jean, *Csaplovics*, author of several statistical and literary works on Hungary, rightly esteemed, *Graeffer*, one of the editors of the *Oesterreichische National-Encyclopädie*. We seize this opportunity with delight to thank Messieurs the librarians and keepers of the different establishments we have visited for their kindnesses and their courtesies that they have shown us, and without whose help we would not have been able to reach the goal we had assigned ourselves in undertaking such a difficult task. We also owe thanks to other scholars already named, and in particular M. de *Hammer*, and to a philologist, who is at the same time one of the best living Slavicists and polyglots, M. *Kopitar*, who was kind enough to review the whole draft of our work and to solve anything we doubted with respect to those parts which are foreign to the sphere of our special studies.

Occupied by literary works of another type in order to fulfill our promises toward the public and to satisfy the commitments contracted with the editor of our *Abrégé de Géographie*, we have not disposed of enough time to extend our research to all the libraries classified in this table. We thought of completing our work by taking advantage of the works of MM. Böckh, Pezzl, Tschischka, and of that which a distinguished statistician, M. Blumenbach, has just published under the title of *Neueste Landeskunde von Oesterreich unter der Ens*. In order to enable the reader to distinguish what belongs to us from that which we have drawn from these works, we have placed an asterisk (*) in front of the names of the libraries, whose number of volumes had been estimated by one of the authors we have just named.

Our framework refuses to expose all the observations we would have to make for the justification of the numbers which we have decided upon. We could draft, for example, relative to the number of volumes of these libraries a table even more stinging than the one we have given at pages 33–41. But we shall restrict ourselves to asking the reader to recall what we have stated about calculating the riches of the

Imperial Library in Vienna and the Royal [Library] of Paris. Positive information taken about the *Library of the Academy of Fine Arts* has convinced us not to assign it a place in this table, despite the thousands of volumes that the best description of Vienna ascribe to it; we know from a good source that it counts only a few hundred.

Statistical Table
of the Principal Libraries of Vienna

Names of the Libraries	*Number of*	
Public Libraries	*Volumes*	*Manuscripts*
Imperial Library	284,000	16,000
Library of the University	102,000	
Private Libraries		
I. Subdivision		
*Library of the Servits	22,000	
*Library of the Augustinians	15,000	
*Library of the Scottish [Benedictines]	13,000	
Library of the Military Archives	22,000[a]	
*Library of the Theresian Academy	30,000	120
Library of the Polytechnical Institute	12,000	
*Library of the Josephine Academy	6,000	
*Library of the Academy of Oriental Languages	3,500[b]	
Library of the Society of Agriculture	2,006	
Library of the Observatory of the University	3,000	
Library of the Philharmonic Society of Austria	2,020[c]	
Library of the Cabinet of Natural History	10,000	
Library of the Numismatic Cabinet	6,000	
Library of the Aulic Chamber	5,000	
Library of the Imperial Archives	2,000[d]	
II. Subdivision		
Library of the late His Majesty Emperor Francis I.	48,000[e]	
Library of His Majesty the young King of Hungary[f]	12,000[g]	
Library of Archduke Charles	25,000[h]	
Library of the late Archduke Antoine	12,000	

[a]*Without the maps and the plans.*
[b]*And 15,000 diplomas, documents, divani, etc.*
[c]*And more than 8,000 musical compositions.*
[d]*Only the printed books.*
[e]*Without the prints and the geographical maps.*
[f]*Presently the reigning emperor, Ferdinand I.*
[g]*Without the prints.*
[h]*Without the prints, the plans and the geographical maps.*

Names of the Libraries	Number of	
	Volumes	*Manuscripts*
III. Subdivision		
Library of Prince Metternich	23,000[a]	
*Library of the Prince of Liechtenstein	40,000	
*Library of Prince Esterhazy	20,000[b]	
Library of the Prince of Dietrichstein	10,000	
Library of the Prince Razoumoffsky	15,000[c]	
Library of the Count of Schönborn	14,000	
Library of Count Fuchs	8,000	
Library of Baron de Bretfeld-Chlumczansky	10,000	
Library of Knight de Hammer	7,500[d]	300
Library of Knight de Kesaer	5,000	
Library of M. Postalaka	2,200	
IV. Subdivision		
Library of the Count of Kolowrat in Reichenau	16,000	
Library of Prince Lobkowitz in Prague	70,000	
Library of Prince Kinsky in Prague	40,000	
Library of the Count of Klebelsberg in Prague	18,000	
Library of the Count of Clam-Martinitz in Prague	21,000	
Library of Prince Lobkowitz in Raudnitz	100,000	1,680
Library of Prince Dietrichstein in Nikolsburg	10,000	650
Library of the Count of Salm in Raitz	20,000	
Library of Count Karoly in Toth-Megyer	18,000	
*Library of the Prince of Schwarzenberg in Krumau	30,000	

[a]*Without the collection of geographical maps.*
[b]*Without the collection of prints.*
[c]*Without the collection of geographical maps and of prints.*
[d]*These figures concern solely the library in Vienna.*

Appendix 1

Statistics of the
General Archives of Venice

Among the national and foreign writers, who, these last years, have described the city of Venice, we do not know of one who has spoken about its *Archives* with the details that this superb establishment deserves. His Majesty, Emperor Francis I., who has been spending* such considerable sums for several years for the restoration of the principal monuments of this city which were about to fall in ruins, for the maintenance of its numerous canals, for the repair and the lengthening of the famous dike, known by the name of *Murazzi*, as well as to recall into its harbor that commerce, which, formerly, made it so rich and so powerful, has just spent 500,000 francs for the centralization of all the archives of the former Republic of Venice and of the governments which succeeded it. This wise and important resolve had as an overlapping goal to gather in one building all the precious documents dispersed in several buildings, so as to facilitate their research and to supervise more easily their conservation, as well as to preserve from destruction, which was threatening them, the vast convent of the Frari and the superb temple which belongs to it. A couple of years has sufficed for the execution of this useful project, and the city of Venice, thanks to this gesture of munificence of His Majesty, can boast today of possessing *the largest archives which exist*, independently of the importance and the rarity of the documents which they contain. We have visited the large archives of *Madrid*, of *Lisbon*, of *Paris* and of *Vienna*; we have gained exact information on those of *Rome*, of *London*, of *Munich*, of *Dresden*, of *Copenhagen* and of several other capitals rightly renowned by these large collections, and all our research has confirmed our opinion, because we do not hesitate to state it: there is not another city which offers in one building such a mass of documents as considerable as the one gathered in the *General Archives* of Venice.

From 1815 to 1834 these sums rose to almost 19,000,000 francs.

Reserving for another article the identification of the most precious documents preserved in this establishment, we shall restrict ourselves now to offer the reader a few positive facts, which shall give him an idea of its immensity.

The *General Archives*, distributed with admirable order, is composed of 298 rooms, salons and hallways, whose walls are covered from top to bottom with shelves. If the latter were joined together and placed one after the other without any interval between them, they would form a straight line which would not have less than 77,238 feet, equivalent to almost fourteen geographical miles — sixty to a degree — or approximately one and a half times the distance from Paris to Versailles. Despite the immensity of this line of shelves, the space was still found to be insufficient to house the 8,664,709 volumes or fascicules, which form the sum total of the documents gathered in this establishment. These eight and a half million volumes belong to 1,809 different archives.

Considering that a part of these documents is very old, and that another part — quite considerable — still goes back to eras rather distant from us; taking into consideration the very different sizes of paper, the forms of the characters — the more complicated, generally speaking, and consequently of a more difficult writing, as they are more ancient, we think we would not be much mistaken if we stated that a thousand writers, who would be working every day, eight hours a day without stopping, would not use up less than 734 years, or 22¼ generations to copy all the documents of these Archives. Thus a thousand persons, who would have started their task when the Crusaders, led by Godefroid de Bouillon, were hoisting their victorious flags on the fortress walls of David's and Solomon's ancient residence, would today barely have been able to finish it.

Supposing that each volume or fascicule contains 80 leaves, and giving each leaf 16 inches of length and 9 inches of width, each one of these unfolded leaves will have the length of one and a half feet. These dimensions and the number of the leaves are far from being exaggerated because we ourselves saw a large number of volumes of 150, 200, 300 and up to 400 leaves. Most of these documents are register-books, all of them large folio size, and moreover we know that almost all the ancient documents were written on large-sized paper, as is the case with the acts of the different governments and the diverse administrations of which these archives are composed. Now then, the 8,664,709 volumes or fascicules contain, after the assumption we have just made, 693,176,720 leaves, or in round numbers 693,200,000 leaves. If all these leaves were opened and placed one after the other, without allowing any interval between them, they would form a band that would measure 1,444,800,000 feet long by 16 inches wide. According to the excellent *Traité d'Astronomie*, which a famous mathematician, M. Littrow, is publishing in Stuttgart, a treatise in which the high theories of that science and all its recent discoveries are made available to everyone, the circumference of the earth taken at the equator is only 123,345,720 feet of Paris. Now then, we have just seen that all the leaves of the *Archives* can form a band of 1,444,800,000 feet long. By dividing therefore the latter figure by the former, we shall obtain as a quotient 11–1/30 approximately, a figure which indicates how many times we could gird the globe with that band at its largest dimension.

If we were to divide by 500 the 693,200,000 leaves, we would obtain 1,386,400 reams, to each one of which, as we have just seen, we could give 16 inches in length and 9 inches in width; we think we could also give them a mean thickness of 6 inches. Now, if we considered all these reams as so many pieces for building purposes, we could erect an enormous pyramid with a square base, whose side would be about 68 feet and its height 428! This pyramid would then be as high as the one of *Cheops*, the largest such monument ever erected by man; equal in volume to several pyramids of the Region of the Nile, it would pass all the others in height! But so as to talk to the reader in terms of objects seen by a larger number of people, we shall add that the volume of our pyramid is equal to the one of the tower of the cathedral of Vienna and almost triple in volume of the belfry of St. Mark in Venice; measures recently taken with the utmost of precision place the elevation of the former at 417 feet and that of the latter 283.

If we wanted to know how many vessels were necessary to transport in one trip all the documents contained in these Archives, we should first attempt to know their weight. However, we already know that they contain 1,386,400 reams. Estimating at 9 pounds the average weight of a ream, we shall have 12,477,600 pounds, which, reduced into tons, the measure used for gauging ships, will give us 6,238 16/20, or in round numbers 6,200 tons. In the table published in 1830 under the title *The World compared with the British Empire* we have given the merchant marine fleet belonging in 1826 to the principal harbors of the British and French Monarchies and that of the Anglo-American Confederation. Going down the column giving the French merchant fleet, we see that in order to transport these Archives we would need more than one-third of the tonnage belonging to the port of *Dunkirk*, half of the one of *Dieppe* and much more than half the tonnage belonging to the ports of *Toulon*, of *Bayonne*, of *Morlaix*, of *Cherbourg*, of *La Rochelle*, of *St. Servan*, of *Granville* and of *Vannes*; that it would be necessary to use all the tonnage of the ports of *Caen*, of *Honfleur* and of *Fécamp,* and almost the whole of the tonnage of all the ports of *Corsica,* while all the vessels belonging to each of the ports of *Cette,* of *Martigues,* of *St. Tropez,* of *Lorient* and of *Sables* would not suffice to execute this transport.

From the dimensions we have given to each leaf, the surface thereof can be evaluated at two square feet. The 693,200,000 leaves will therefore have 1,386,400,000 square feet. In the article we have published in the *Gazzetta Privilegiata di Milano* Nr. 62, 63, 64 and 65 of 1834 on the number of Jews presently alive, we have seen that the total population of the globe can today be estimated at 745 million souls. Granting two square feet to each individual, only 1,590 million of these feet would be necessary to line them up one next to the other. But considering that more than one-third of the people presently alive have not reached their full development, we shall be able to reduce the 1,590 millions to 1,300 only. We have seen above that all the leaves of the Archives offer a surface of 1,368,400,000 square feet. Thus the whole human race presently alive could be comfortably installed on the leaves contained in the Archives of Venice!

Each leaf being covered with writing on both sides, to have the total surface covered with writing of the documents of these Archives we must double the one we have obtained when considering only one side of the paper. By multiplying by two, therefore, the 1,386,400,000 square feet, we shall have 2,772,800,000 and in round numbers 2,273 million square feet. Now then, an Italian square mile of 60 to a degree at the equator containing 32,609,810¼ square feet of Paris, these 2,773 million square feet will equal to a little more than 85 of these square miles. Now, opening our *Abrégé de Géographie* or our *Bilancia Politica del Globo,* where the surface of all the states of Europe and of America and that of the principal states of the other parts of the world is calculated in these same square miles and according to the best sources, we find that the *totality of the written surface* of the documents kept in the Archives of Venice is almost sevenfold the surface of the *Seigniory of Kniphausen** and fivefold that of the *Republic of San*

Here are the surface areas of the countries named in the text:

Names of the States or Countries	Surface in square miles of 60 to a degree
Seigniory of Kniphausen	*13*
Republic of San Marino	*17*
Principality of Monaco	*38*
Principality of Liechtenstein	*40*
Republic of Bremen	*51*
Canton of Zug	*64*
Republic of Frankfurt and Canton of Geneva	*69*

Marino; twofold the superficy of the *Principalities of Monaco and of Liechtenstein*; it exceeds by far the territories of the *Republic of Bremen*, of the *Canton of Zug*, of the *Republic of Frankfurt* and of the *Canton of Geneva*; that it is larger than the *Principality of Hohenzollern-Hechingen* and than *Columbia* or the *Federal District*, which contains the capital of the Anglo-American Confederation; that it is almost equal to the *Canton of Schaffhouse*, to the *Republic of Lübeck*, while it is a little smaller than the *Principalities of Reuss-Schleiz* (less Gera) and of *Reuss-Greiz*, than the *Republic of Hamburg*, than the *Canton of Appenzell* and than the *Landgrève of Hesse-Homburg*. We shall finish these comparisons by observing that the written surface of these Archives equals more than half the surface of the *Department of the Seine*, which contains Paris, and more than one-third the surface of the *County of Middlesex* to which belongs four-fifths of the City of London, which, today, seems to us to be exceeding in spread and population all the cities of the world.

(cont.)

Names of the States or Countries	Surface in square miles of 60 to a degree
Principality of Hohenzollern-Hechingen	82
Columbia or the Federal District of the United States	75
Canton of Schaffhouse	86
Republic of Lübeck	88
Reuss-Schleiz without the Principality of Gera	98
Principality of Reuss-Greiz	109
Republic of Hamburg	114
Canton of Appenzell	115
Landgrève of Hesse-Homburg	125
Seine Department	138
County of Middlesex	212

Appendix 2

On the Political Importance of the Austrian Monarchy, on Emperor Francis I, and on the Progress of Civilization in the Empire of Austria

Among the large number of remarkable passages that we could cite, we shall restrict ourselves to the following ones; we borrow the first ones from the *Notices Politiques et Littéraires sur l'Allemagne* which a conscientious, eloquent and fervent author, M. Saint-Marc Girardin, has just published in Paris; we shall draw the others from the *Revue Britannique*, a journal rightly renowned among all the notables of the civilized world, in which, since 1825, trained and scholarly French pens reproduce, always with remarkable talent and sometimes even improving on that, the substance of the most important articles of the British reviews and journals, so rich in stimulating facts and in new and philosophical views. Being only a simple reporter, we shall reproduce faithfully these passages as we find them, despite a few errors in the details we have noticed in them and which could not be entirely avoided by authors who write so far away from the locales that form the subject of their profound meditations.

At page 38 M. Sainte-Marc Girardin says: "There is no country which is judged with as much disfavor as Austria, and there is not any which cares less about it. Austria feels aversion for publicity to such an extent as to not wish for any praise. Praise offends her as much as blame. Because the one who praises today may blame tomorrow: to tolerate being praised is to fall into the claws of discussion. Now then, Austria does not wish any discussion: she has the cult of the religion of silence, and that religion goes almost as far as fanaticism. In this way Austria has educational establishments worthy of serving as models: she does not breathe a word about them. She is, after England, the first state in Europe to have built railroads: no one has heard a word about them. It has a just, equitable, active administration which has nothing of the feudal nor of the aristocratic, a liberal administration created by Joseph II.: she has made no ado about it; an excellent civil code: she does not boast about it. Her motto is to hide the good even, as much as possible to get rid of the spirit of scrutiny and of discussion.

"Do not believe that Austria, inheriting the politics of Venice as she has inherited from her states, precipitates her people into pleasures in order to divert them from politics and that she favors immorality as a useful distraction. No: Austria watches over the mores of the people and believes that in any event an honest people is easier to govern than a licentious and corrupted one. To maintain the good mores of the people, Austria does not solely rely on the clergy's care: she favors popular instruction and believes that instruction is the helper of good morals. In Austria the children of the people are all compelled to attend school and they are not allowed to marry unless they can show a school certificate. Education, which tends to form good farmers and good workers, tradespeople and manufacturers, chemists, mathematicians, engineers, doctors of medicine, education, which has for its goal the practice of arts useful to life, is favored and propagated in all possible ways. Education, which has for its goal to form men of letters, attorneys, philosophers, education which teaches to reason, to criticize, to discuss, is restricted and withheld.

"Austria does not fear truth; she fears doubt and scrutiny which do their best to shake things up, truth as well as lies. Here is an anecdote which can show that Austria does not fear truth as long as it is a truth which is outside of the circle of disputes, such as the truths of history or those which science discovers through experience. Napoleon, during his reign, had ordered built in Milan, a triumphal arch and he had ordered the bas-reliefs that were to adorn the four sides of that arch. One of these bas-reliefs represented, in a humiliated posture, Emperor Francis receiving the peace from Napoleon. The triumphal arch was barely springing out of the ground when Napoleon died. Emperor Francis ordered the work continued and the bas-reliefs executed according to the orders received from Bonaparte. These bas-reliefs were put into place a year ago, I believe. However, so that this history lesson be complete, other bas-reliefs, placed next to the first ones, represented Emperor Francis entering his capital triumphant after the defeat of Napoleon. I know that the Austrian government has no other merit in all this than to uphold the historical truth, but all the governments do not have this respect for history. In order to have it, one must have faith in oneself, one must believe in one's strength and in its duration, one must feel oneself above the political vicissitudes and rely on one's rights — which cannot pass nor change — rather than good fortune, which is always on the move and vain.

"No State has, to as good a degree, more reason than Austria to have faith in its force and its duration. Twice she has seen her capital visited by enemy armies, twice her power has been thrown asunder and as if smashed to pieces, twice the enemy (and what an enemy! France, with its turbulent ideas and its innovating mind) has promenaded freely in her cities and her countryside. Well! after all these misfortunes, Austria rose back out of her ashes, and as she was arising has found herself the way she had always been. The invasion of France, in 1814, caused a revolution: the double invasion of Austria caused no revolution. She underwent the shakeups of conquest but she does not know the shakeups of revolutions. This stability of the empire during great catastrophes is a remarkable trait; it is a remarkable trait indeed for any nation, which stands steadfast against changing its laws and its governments, which sees innovations pass by without adopting a single one of them, which clings together with its princes in the latter's misfortunes, suffers with them, and draws, from that communion of misfortunes, a more vivid and more profound affection.

"The people love the emperor as a son loves his father, and the emperor, in turn, by his vigilance, by his laborious zeal and especially by the sweet simplicity of his manners, tries to deserve the love of the people. The imperial family does not know etiquette. Often the emperor promenades on foot, followed by an aide-de-camp. It is during one of these promenades, at Schönbrunn, during the cholera epidemic, that, encountering a coffin that was being carried to the cemetery, without anyone accompanying it on its last trip, he asked why this coffin was thusly abandoned. 'It is most probably some poor soul who has neither relatives nor friends,' replied the aide-de-camp. 'Well! We shall follow it ourselves, if you wish,' said the emperor; and lowering his hat, he accompanied the coffin all the way to the cemetery, threw the first shovelful on the tomb and went home. For an absolute sovereign, is that not understanding true human equality in a touching manner?

"If I am to believe all the unanimous tales from Vienna, the emperor has not only the virtues that make princes beloved ones, but also the talent which makes them reign; he is industrious, active, vigilant. This prince, which we imagine, I do not know why, as some sort of medieval 'do-nothing' king, works twelve hours a day and knows all the languages and the patois of his empire. Every Wednesday he receives whomsoever wishes to talk to him. Peasants from all the parts of the empire come to these audiences, without introductory letter, without tickets, but with a simple number, which assigns them their turn and which is distributed to them in the antechamber; they enter into the emperor's cabinet, remain one to one with him and present

their business to him. It is rare for peasants from the hereditary States
to enter into a suit without first consulting the emperor. It is said that
to this rule can be added that in case of a dispute between a lord and a
peasant, the lord should be triply right to win his suit."

At page 43, M. Saint-Marc Girardin says: "By its discretion
alone, the Austrian government is already some sort of prodigy in our
Europe, which is everywhere open to news and to gossip. In France, in
England, the government is a perpetual dialogue between the people
and the authorities. In Austria neither the authorities nor the people
say a word. Such is the Austrian government, as serious, as silent, as
steadfast in the middle of a vacillating Europe as the Egyptian sphinx:

> Among these mounts of burning and shifting sands,
> What are the winds' whims doing and undoing!*

"There exists a singular accord between the mores of Austria
and its destiny. Prussia loves to multiply its surroundings because it
must make its fortune, and touching everything is a means of
encroaching on anything. Austria seems to have multiplied her surroundings only to multiply her chances at mediation. Placed in the
middle of Europe she is touching France through Switzerland and
Piedmont, the whole of Germany through Bohemia, Russia through
the Polish provinces, finally the Orient through Hungary. In this
fashion, wherever there may be a shock or some agitation, anywhere
there exists a fear that Europe may be on the move, Austria carries all
her weight thereto, in order to establish a balance of power and to re-
establish order. Not a single State enjoys a geographical location which
could improve its political vocation better.

"There are powers which have the initiative of movement.
Austria has, in Europe, the initiative of order and of steadiness. Other
powers are the wind which pushes the ships across the oceans; Austria
is their ballast; it maintains the ship; it prevents its ever oscillating in a
dangerous fashion. I do not know whether Europe could do better
without France, which gives the chariot of civilization its impetus, than
without Austria, which maintains it in its orbit. With France as sole
leader, civilization would soon be torn away toward the abyss; with
Austria, it would not move. Civilization needs both forces: it needs the
force that pushes and it needs the force that holds it back: it is at that
price only that its march can be rapid without endangering its stead-
fastness.

"Take a look at the history of Austria since Rudolph of

*Chapelain, la Pucelle, ch. 1.

Hapsburg. Placed at the rearguard of Europe, it is she who checks the impulse of the minds; she resists the innovations; but this resistance is useful to the innovations themselves. She gives time to examine them, to control them, to correct them. For innovations to succeed, they must undergo a long noviciate of experiments and trials. Austria, by her resistance, helps this necessary noviciate. She has resisted Protestantism in the Thirty Years War, as she has resisted the French Revolution in the last wars: she has prevented Europe from adopting with confidence the Protestant system and the French system. They are services which she rendered to civilization. Because Protestantism in 1648, at the Peace of Westphalia, was better than in those beginnings, and the political philosophy of '89 is without a doubt better today than in '93. How have these two systems improved? Because they have been fought, because they have satisfied their noviciate of experiments, because they have learnt during this 'apprenticeship' to take the natures of man and of society into account; it is only at that price that they have been salutary to civilization. Nothing resembles less the artful work of civilization than the excessive effort of the systemic spirit. Civilization does not reject in a lump all the constitutions and all the opinions of past centuries; there are those which it admits, there are those which it rejects. Each time that a new system is wont to get a hold of Europe, the vocation of Austria is to give civilization the time to sort things out between the past and the future; such is her destiny, such is her role in the drama of European history, a more useful role than it is a brilliant one."

At page 313 of the Fifth Volume of the Third Series of the *Revue Britannique*, published in 1833, we find the following passage in a remarkable article on the *progress of civilization in the Austrian possessions*:

"Spain and Portugal excepted, there is not a single one of the absolute governments of Europe which, in the course of these last years, has devoted the greatest care in increasing the material welfare of the lower classes. In that respect see what the Court itself has attempted. We are not, by far, partisans of the absolute system; but we cannot refrain from observing the existence of an incontestable fact. To be certain, it will not be thought that the Austrian government is moved by a very good will in favor of Italy and toward the other States that it has added to the hereditary domains by the force of weapons; nonetheless, it has done more for the physical and moral welfare of all these peoples than most of the constitutional governments of Europe; but it has showered these good deeds without ado, without hiring these thousands of trumpets of Fame to vaunt its work. So what. Many people, today, believe with the best faith in the world, that the improvement of the lot of nations can only be achieved through the press; they need sensation, sudden uproar and smoke: without all these vain accessories there is no improvement possible in their view: this is yet another error.

"In half a century the condition of the peoples which are under the domination of the House of Austria has entirely changed in aspect; and it is with the greatest injustice that some travelers contend that this vast empire has remained stationary. In order to be well convinced of the happy turnabout that has taken place in this State, one should only cast a glance on the present situation of the industry in High and Low Austria, in Bohemia, in Moravia and in the diverse cantons of the Tyrol and of Styria. Where fifty years ago you were seeing only thatched huts, a few rare herds or poachers, today numerous factories have arisen, metallurgical works are in full exploitation and the most marvelous products of all these industries are produced. If from the Mediterranean countries you pass to the Littoral: lighthouses strewn with profusion on the coasts of the Mediterranean and the Adriatic, the activity in the harbors of Trieste, of Venice, of Fiume, the one of Ragusa, of Spalatro and of Cattaro in Dalmatia, the bustle which reigns in the port of Rovigno, in Istria, all those attest to this immense development. One can easily understand that commerce and the manufacturing industries cannot prosper within a State without spreading their progress to agriculture. And that is precisely what has happened to that important sector of industry in Austria; but, it must be said, nothing on the part of the government has been neglected during the last years to hasten its development. Harrach has witnessed the rise of a magnificent pomological establishment; some schools for perfecting agriculture and the veterinary art, under the title of *Georgicon* were formed in Altenburg, in Kessthely, in Etska; to favor the study of exotic plants and their acclimatization Archduke Rainier has created and enriched with his gifts the botanical garden of Monza, while, thanks to the munificence of the emperor and of his august brothers, model farms and botanical gardens have sprung up recently in the vicinity of Vienna and in several parts of the Empire. But every bit as soon as a government has engaged itself on the road of progress, it cannot resist this powerful force which drags it relentlessly forward: therefore the sciences and the fine arts have not tarried in receiving their part of the impulse.

"Observatories and schools of astronomy have been created in the most suitable places for the study of the skies; Innsbruck and Graez have witnessed the opening of two very remarkable museums; the academies of fine arts of Vienna, of Milan and of Venice have been founded or reorganized with an eye on propagating painting, sculpture and the art of drawing, while in the navy schools of Trieste and Venice, and in the military schools of Neustadt, of Vienna and of Olmutz, all newly founded, a young elite destined to carry instruction into the ranks of the army is being educated under a system of severe courses. Views of immediate usefulness, of the future and of prosperity have also prompted the Austrian government to create two polytechnic schools in Vienna and in Prague and a school of mines in Chemnitz, which have produced for it these excellent engineers, who, in just a few years, have executed the cadastral survey and the triangulation of the whole empire, immense operations if one considers that Austria has a perimeter of 4,000 geographical miles. But how can the many works of public usefulness that have been undertaken everywhere be described, how can one identify the multitude of bridges that have been thrown across impetuous rivers, how can one sketch the numerous ramifications of this internal navigation, which is composed of more than three hundred canals as well as that immense network of macadamized roads thrown over the entire surface of the Empire, and of which rival those that Napoleon had laid on Mount Cenis and the Simplon. Here is the draining of the vast marshes of Laybach, the magnificent hydraulic works of Weinerisch-Neustadt, of Banat and of Pavia; here the railroads of Upper Austria and of Bohemia; here coaches and steamboats, suspended bridges in iron or in steel thrown across the Danube and Dniester, which are telltale enough about the fact that the Austrian government is not out of touch with a single discovery, with a single improvement.

"We repeat it: it is not the apology of the Austrian government that we have wanted to present here; we are neither the partisans of its meticulous and preventive policy nor of the ambitious pretentions of the House of Lorraine-Austria; however, we take it to heart to signal progress where it exists because this equitable appreciation permits us to be severe every time we find something to recriminate. But, when outside of the large enterprises of public usefulness, which we have just enumerated, we see that the Austrian government, in these last fifteen years, has spread to all the communes of its vast empire the benefits of elementary education, when we see that in this short span of time it has founded or reorganized a large number of universities, that it has created two hundred gymnasiums, a hundred thirty colleges, eighty seminaries, twenty-five lycaeums, twelve courses of philosophy, five chairs of statistics, etc., we cannot refrain from stating that such a government really works for the welfare of its subjects, and that it is unjust, despite the power without control that it has arrogated to itself, to accuse it of being the enemy of enlightenment."

At page 323 the anonymous author concludes his article by the following remarkable passage: "Thus, everywhere in Europe, and whatever form the governments may have, the human race is on the go: at St. Petersburg, at Constantinople, as in London, as in Paris; and with all due deference to our prejudices, in this large arena of civilization, it is not Austria that trails."

Appendix 3

Anecdotes About Emperor Francis I

We borrow from No. 1986 of the *Temps*, one of the principal organs of the French periodic press, the following anecdotes about Emperor Francis I. It is a shining homage rendered to his memory and a new proof of impartiality, which advantageously distinguishes this political and literary journal, in which we find so often articles on all the disciplines of human knowledge edited with a remarkable talent.

"In 1833, Francis I. was in Prague. His popular audiences held their course, there as in Vienna. One day, an old and poor woman appeared in tears. She could barely make herself clear: sobs were choking her. The Emperor encouraged her with kind words and obtained the story of the sorrows that tormented her. She was an itinerant musician: her hurdy-gurdy was her only fortune. But what was she going to become now that her hurdy-gurdy was broken? She needed five florins to have it repaired. 'Five florins,' she sighed! 'The sum is considerable and, without the necessary repairs, my hurdy-gurdy remains useless. I can no longer earn my living.' 'If it is only that,' said the Emperor; and he put a sum of money in the hand of the musician. The latter withdrew, thanking her august benefactor; but before reaching the door, she has had the time to count the money. 'Sire,' says she as she turns around, 'there are ten florins and I need only five. Take back the remainder.' 'Keep it all my good woman, because your hurdy-gurdy may again be out of order and I shall not always be on hand to repair the damage.'

"A few days later it was an old soldier's turn. He wanted only to tell the Emperor that his pension of 4 kreutzers per day sufficed at most to keep him away from the pangs of hunger, and that, if it should not displease His Majesty, he would like to spread it thick just once. The request was too modest to be refused. Francis I. drew a coin of 20 kreutzers from his purse and gave it to the veteran. Surprised but not discontented our man beat in retreat. However, on the threshold he is stopped by the voice of the Prince. 'Well! old fellow, is it enough?' 'A poor devil like I is happy with anything.' 'In that case, and because it pleased you, I warn you that starting immediately, every day you will receive such a coin of 20 kreutzers.' Be the judge of the soldier's joy!

"In 1815, when Francis I. visited the Tyrol for the first time his affable manners won him all the hearts. The day after his arrival at Innsbruck, he spent the whole day receiving those who presented themselves. Finally, toward ten o'clock, exhausted from fatigue and speaking, he left the room of the audience to seek some rest and supper in his interior apartments. But he was not at the end of his troubles. He was indeed warned that there remained three mountaineers still in the antechamber and asking to be admitted. Then, forgetting the meal which was awaiting him he stepped their way, saying: 'Truly, if they are sitting over there, waiting for me, I just must go and fetch them.' The testimonials of love which surrounded him everywhere, in this country so famous for its chivalrous loyalty touched him deeply. 'It is well that I did not come any earlier in the Tyrol. Oh! if I had known how much I was loved here, the loss of this province would have been a sorrow too much above my strength.'

"One time they admitted to him a calligrapher who had represented, by means of artistically enlaced strokes, the double eagle of Austria. Each feather which composed the wings contained a motto written in such a delicate writing that it was impossible to decipher them with the naked eye. The good Emperor admired cordially this masterpiece of patience; but he wanted to know the meaning of all the words that the complicated coils of the drawing were concealing. They were emphatic compliments, in which the governmental virtues of the Prince were pompously exalted. As the writer advanced in his reading, Francis manifested an increasingly pronounced impatience because he recognized in this exaggerated style the language of flattery and not the one of love. Finally, beyond endurance, he handed his gift to the reader and sent him off with these few words: 'Take because you are an artful artist; but I would have rewarded more amply and more cordially if you had not played the role of a courtier.'

"A young man of a good family approached the Emperor for a position which had been refused him elsewhere. Pretending long studies and extensive acquired knowledge, he claimed to be suited for a diplomatic career because he understood and spoke most of the dead or living languages. According to him, hatred and partiality of his enemies had been the only obstacles to his advancement. Immediately Francis I. interrogated him in Latin, then in Italian and finally in French. The young man remained mute. 'It is possible,' said the Emperor after a few minutes of waiting, 'that on the spur of the moment you may not have mastered all the assurance necessary to display your means. Let us see,' added he, with kindness, 'put your mind at ease and formulate for me in any of the three languages I have used, at your choice, your request.'

The he turned toward other people present and came back to the young solicitor only after a long tour all around the apartment. But then, still the same silence. 'This is too much,' exclaimed the Emperor severely. 'Not only have you boasted of talents you do not possess, but you have calumniated people whose only misdeed was to have judged you correctly. Go and make certain I do not ever again encounter you.' "

Appendix 4

Comparison of the Population of Paris with That of Vienna According to the Census of 1832

Here are the elements of which the populations of these two large capitals were composed in the year 1832. We borrow those of Vienna from the *Statistique officielle*, which since 1829 is presented every year to His Majesty the Emperor; we have drawn those of Paris from the remarkable work which the elite of the French statisticians has just published under the title *Rapport sur la marche et les effets du choléra-morbus dans Paris et le département de la Seine.* Figures adopted by MM. Villermé, Benoiston de Chateauneuf and Villot as a basis for their nice work deserve the highest confidence and must be preferred over any other evaluation which could be put up against them. The conscientious research, done by these famous statisticians in order to know as precisely as possible the population count of that metropolis at the time of the invasion of this terrible plague, has convinced us to adopt their evaluation with finality, no matter how much different it may have been from the one adopted in our preceding works. We shall explain in another work how the population of Paris, which an official document carried to 890,304 in 1826, found itself reduced to 785,862 at the end of 1831.

The population of Vienna in the beginning of 1832 stood at 339,787 souls.

In that number 316,417 belonged to the civilian status, 23,370 belonged to the military status.

Among the 316,417 civilian inhabitants, 150,672 belonged to the male sex and 165,745 to the female sex. In the same number 13,977 foreigners were counted.

The population of Paris, in the beginning of 1832, stood at 785,862 souls. In that number 753,987 persons were counted in their residence; 366,411 belonged to the masculine sex and 387,576 belonged to the female sex.

A total of 31,875 persons were counted outside of their residence, to wit: 15,576 soldiers; 2,665 in the civilian prisons; 8,272 in the civilian hospices and 5,362 in the civilian hospitals.

To have truly comparable elements between these two capitals, we must deduct the foreigners and the soldiers respectively. We find that in the report on the cholera the average population of furnished hotels is being evaluated and that it can be considered as equivalent to the number of foreigners, from 35,000 to 40,000 and that of the soldiers at 15,576. These two sums form in round numbers 53,000. By deducting this figure from the 785,862, we find 733,000, which will be the civilian and permanent population of Paris at the time indicated. The same subtractions will give us for Vienna, at the same time 302,000 inhabitants. The populations of these two capitals will therefore be like 733,000 to 302,000, or like 246 to 100, or like about *five* to *two*.

Statistical Summary of the Technological Collection of His Majesty the Emperor Ferdinand I

"The manufacturing industry," says M. Adolphe Blanqui,* "consists in giving to raw or already fashioned materials a value which they did not have by modifying them in such a way as to render them useful. This industry embraces the whole physical world; it begins with the simplest of operations and finishes with the most complicated: its power appears sometimes with as much grandeur in the smallest details as in the most gigantic enterprises. I also admire its processes when it transforms a bar of copper into pins, and when it changes into mirrors or into crystals the sand of our dunes and the soda drawn from the lost marine plants on our beaches. The agricultural industry is limited by the extent of territory: the manufacturing industry knows for limits only those of the genius of mankind. Through it we have seen populations almost devoid of arable lands obtain all that can satisfy their needs and even the enjoyments of life: Geneva has for a long time exchanged the sole products of its watchmaking for the products of Europe. With thrift and order an industrious nation increases its capital indefinitely, and, as a result, the scope of its manufacturing operations.

"By means of the manufacturing industry the most base materials have been provided with an immense usefulness. The rags, waste of our households, have been transformed into white and light sheets of paper, which carry the commercial orders and the processes of the arts to the confines of the world. Depositories of the concepts of genius, they transmit the experiences of the centuries down to us. They safeguard the titles to our properties, we entrust them with the noblest and most touching feelings of the heart, and we stir up similar senti-

---

*In his excellent Précis élémentaire d'économie politique, in which this young professor has summarized, with a remarkable talent and always with eloquence, the principles of this science, established by the famous economists A. Smith, Say and Ricardo.

ments in the hearts of our fellow men through them. By facilitating to an inconceivable point all the communications of men between them, paper must be considered as one of the products that has most improved the lot of our species.

"We know the wonders accomplished by the manufacturing industry ever since peace has allowed the enlightened nations of the Two Worlds to apply themselves to it with perseverence and security. New products, of any type, have been brought to the market at prices hitherto unknown; the poor man has been able to find in his work sufficient resources not only to exist but also to secure some pleasure, and the inventory of the wealth of the human race surpasses today whatever the most brilliant and most admirable statistics have ever offered. These comforting results are due to progress achieved by enlightenment and industry. Indeed, the works of the manufacturing industry not being limited, as I have shown above, by the extent of territory, it depends on mankind to multiply its products at its will. The experiments that it requires keep capital tied up for a shorter period than does agriculture and the profits it generates are simultaneously more rapid and considerable. The *outlets* are also easier and more numerous: wheat from Sicily and Odessa, wines from Portugal and Burgundy cannot multiply indefinitely nor be sold anywhere while the silk factories of Lyon and the cutlery shops of Birmingham spread through both continents and find buyers. England was buying its hardware from the Germans during the reign of Charles I., and now it furnishes a part of Europe and the whole of South America with it. What a solemn encouragement for hard-working nations! and what future opens itself before them just as soon as they will understand that products are only bought by other products and that work, the primary source of riches, is a thousand times more productive than the mines of Golconde!"

The two sciences which enlighten the principal operations of industry, chemistry and mechanics, have carried their torch into the workshops. In a very few years we have witnessed all kinds of hardware being manufactured by the main civilized nations of Europe, the numerous fabrics of cotton and wool imitated — which, formerly, were the exclusive prerogative of India or England — all the acids produced, soda extracted from marine salt, fabrics of linen being bleached as well as those of cotton and hemp through more economical and faster methods, alum, vitriol and ammonium salts being formed by the direct combination of their component principles, new apparatus for the distillation of wines created, Prussian blue being applied to silk, cochineal replaced by madder root, indigo of anil by those of pastel, cane sugar by beet and potato sugar, vinegar being extracted from wood and this acid being applied to all its ordinary usages.

In this honorable arena of industry, which today is involving almost all the nations of Europe, several regions of the Austrian Empire not only have not remained behind the other states but one can say that they have kept pace with the most hard-working nations, if only the most manufacture-bent cantons of England, France and Belgium are excepted. Bohemia, Moravia, Lower and Upper Austria, Styria and the Lombardo-Venetian kingdom have especially distinguished themselves by their progress in several branches of industry. Cloth, cotton fabrics, ironworks, steelworks, bronzeworks, cabinet-making, glass products, porcelain, jewelry works, musical and optical instruments, hardware and cutlery are the articles which offer the greatest improvements. At the same time an agricultural and manufacturing power, the Empire of Austria belongs to that small number of privileged nations which can, so to speak, be self-sufficient. It is to the various accidents in its vast and fertile territory and to the large difference which can be observed in the climate of its provinces that the Austrian Monarchy owes its great variety of productions. The agricultural and mineral wealth of the least advanced provinces in industry furnish the raw materials to those which distinguish themselves by a hard-working and business-oriented population. A more or less perfected agriculture furnishes abundantly whatever is necessary to the subsistence of its numerous inhabitants, and its manufacturing plants and factories pour into the consumer area all the luxury and all the needs which the rich and the poor, respectively, might require.

Today, when it is generally recognized that commerce, agriculture and the manufacturing industry are the main elements which constitute the strength and the wealth of a nation, governments have more or less been eager to protect them, to encourage them. Therefore, the august Monarch, who has just been laid to rest, encouraged them by all possible means, despite the difficult circumstances into which he had often been plunged during his long and memorable reign. The Prince, who has succeeded him and who takes to heart his noble example, was well imbued with these truths when, during his youth, he devoted to their study and to their application all the leisure that occupations of another type allowed him.

Already in 1819, as he was seeing the impetus of industry in the Empire, the hereditary Prince conceived the project of forming a collection of technology involving all the raw and manufactured products of the different provinces of the Empire as well as the main machines which serve in their making or in their transport. Seconded by a distinguished technologist, by M. Kees,* he succeeded in a few years in

*M. Kees is the author of a classical work published from 1819 to 1823 under the

forming the most considerable and best organized technological collection that exists. At least, that is what we believe we can ascertain by
comparing it with those that we ourselves have had the opportunity to
inspect and by what we have learned about it from competent judges,
who have seen the largest collections of this genre. This collection,
offering all the products of industry arranged after the most remarkable
factories, depending on the successive importance of the improvements
of the latter during the last sixteen years, as well as grouped under the
different provinces of the Monarchy, is, for the state and for the one
who governs it, of the utmost importance. True thermometer of the
activities of the inhabitants of the different provinces and of their
progress in the factories and manufacturing plants, it offers to the
enlightened Prince who formed it the faithful table of the progress of
industry in each one of them; it indicates to him everything that has
been done in the last years to encourage it; it informs him on the
improvements and perfections which are susceptible of occurring in
certain sectors and in certain regions while, simultaneously, it lets him
observe which countries are distinguishing themselves most by their
increasing prosperity. This collection, which for the past sixteen years
has meant a pleasant and useful form of recreation to the heir to the
Crown, during his moments of leisure, formed the nicest decoration of
his apartment. We shall add that its methodical catalogue and the
admirable order with which it is arranged are the result of the special
instructions given directly by its creator.

This magnificent collection is composed of three main parts, to
wit:

    I. Raw Materials
    II. Worked Materials
    III. Models

I. Collection of the Raw Materials

It embraces all the primary materials either entirely raw or only
partially worked, which supply the indigenous factories and manufacturing plants; consequently, it contains also a few articles which are
imported into the Empire and which are indispensable to its manufacturers and its confectioners. The all-encompassing number of the

articles of which it is composed amounts to about 3,500. They are divided according to the three kingdoms of nature. One sees there: wood, flax, raw and prepared hemp of all the countries of the Empire next to the materials which it was intended to replace; cotton of all the qualities, wool and all the hair of animals that is used in the manufacturing plants, the metals, the soils, the stones, etc., etc.

II. Collection of Worked Materials

So far, it is composed only of those products of indigenous industry but we are assured that in the future it will embrace also those of the industries of the other states. The number of articles which it contained was about 38,000 in the beginning of 1835. Here are its most remarkable subdivisions:

Hides: from the totally unprocessed, in use in Istria and the outer military posts, to the finest skins, offering in their long series a host of various articles.

Threads: of flax, of hemp, of silk, of cotton and of wool, either spun by hand or by machines. Of especial mention is the thread for lace worked in Bohemia.

Linens: They are one of the main products of the Monarchy; one can see all the kinds and qualities which enter the trade, from the roughest fabrics of which bags are made to the finest cambrics, either bleached, unbleached, dyed and printed.

Cotton fabrics: Worked in several countries of the Monarchy they can be seen here in all their possible nuances which art and fashions have been able to give them; the chronological arrangement which was given to the samples indicates the progress of the former and the evolution of the latter.

Cloths and silk fabrics: The progress achieved by their manufacture can be noticed perceptibly. The shawls and their edgings distinguish themselves by their beauty and by their low price. Carpets also deserve special mention.

Passementerie: Its articles form several subdivisions, of which the more numerous one is that of silken ribbons; the strings and lace are of a remarkable beauty.

Plait and fabrics in straw and bark: from several parts of the Empire. Those made with machinery surpass in beauty and in low price all the corresponding products which are handmade. We should not forget the works made from *Poa pratensis.*

Papers: This numerous subdivision offers the products of all the principal paper mills of the Empire. One can find among them paper sans-fin, paper of straw and of turf as well as wallpapers, painted and printed papers and playing cards.

Glassware: It is one of the richest and most beautiful subdivisions; it offers items which can be ranked among the masterpieces of the art of the glassmaker. The products of the glassworks of Bohemia especially form a numerous series of articles remarkable by their variety and above all by the elegance of their forms and by the quality of the material; they convey a high idea of the state of perfection to which this industry has arisen in this kingdom. All the new inventions are represented in it by corresponding items; of special mention is the carved glasses collection. In addition to the true vases in glass, this subdivision embraces also painting on glass, optical glass, artistic products of the glassmaker, pearls in glass, artificial gems, the masses of composition and the pieces for glass mosaics, the masses for enamel, mirrors and a host of other articles.

Metals: Is yet another subdivision which comprises the largest number of manufactured items. Copper, brass and tombac in leaves and in wire, and the works in iron and in steel, ranked according to the legal divisions existing in the Austrian Monarchy, offer a prodigious number of articles, of which several are remarkable for the way in which they have been worked. Several are in their natural size; a large number are in reduced proportions.

Pottery: It is here that one finds the countless successions of vases invented until present to satisfy life's exigencies and fashion's caprices, from the most common pots to items in porcelain of the greatest richness and of the most exquisite work.

The smallest subdivisions are not less interesting; a host of objects can be found in them, such as compositions in wood, in cane, in bone, and in horn [ivory]; the works of the cobbler, of the tailor, oil-cloths, waxed silk, artificial flowers, products of the feather dealers, sugar, tobacco, and a large number of others.

The following table, which we were fortunate enough to acquire, can be considered as the statistics of the collection because it contains the number of items included in each of its main subdivisions. It functions as a complement to the brief indications which we have just given on those which appear to us as offering the greatest interest. The articles contained in the table alone exceed the sum of 30,000.

Statistical Table
of the Articles Contained in the Principal Subdivisions

Names of the Subdivisions	*Number of the articles*
Hat trade (millinery)	80
Skins (Pelts)	800
Threads of flax and of hemp	375
Threads of cotton	750
Threads of wool	348
Spun and twisted silk	412
Cloth of flax and of hemp	930
Cloth and fabrics of cotton	5,100
Cloth and fabrics of wool	770
Fabrics of silk	3,250
Fabrics of half-silk and shawls	1,980
Fabrics half flax and half cotton	354
Carpets	76
Passementerie: Works made mechanically	2,613
Handmade works	120
Knitted goods	205
Ropes	194
Strings, lace, etc.	185
Plait and items of straw and bark	354
Paper, white or tinted	912
Paper, colored, printed and with imprints	1,519
Wallpaper	805
Playing cards	105
Engravings on wood	36
Lithography	166
Engravings on copper and on steel	125
Printing	77
Compositions on wood, reed, bone, horn, etc.	813
Glove items	91
Shoemaking articles	62
Saddlery articles and leatherworks	35
Oil cloths and waxed silks	104
Artificial flowers	127
Articles of feather dealers	59
Sugar products	134
Tobacco	78
Copper, brass and similor or tombac in leaves	146
Copper, brass and similor in wires	375
Imprints on metals	340
Metal buttons	750
Molten brass items	103
Molten iron items	156
Plate in iron and steel	95
Files	314
Cutlery	217
Scythes, etc.	71
Horsehoes and other articles from the smith	78
Other articles in iron	1,500

Names of the Subdivisions	*Number of the articles*
Bricks	66
Ordinary pottery	101
Black ordinary pottery	32
Ordinary crockery	17
Fine crockery	182
Vases in stone and crucibles	53
Porcelain	207
Ordinary glassware in general	321
Painted and gilded glassware	63
Glass trinkets and small articles in blown glass	207
Pearls (beads) in glass and artificial gems	1,315
Pastes and pieces for mosaics	326
Pastes for enameling	50
Mirrors	22
Paints	348

III. Collection of Models

It is composed of more than 150 models perfectly well worked and executed with the greatest care on the originals. They are divided into seven classes, to wit:

1. Machines and instruments for the comfort and the security of man.
2. Utensils of rural economy, instruments and machinery related to that important art.
3. Machines and instruments for the exploitation of mines.
4. Technical machines and instruments.
5. Machines and instruments related to civilian architecture.
6. Machines and instruments related to hydraulic architecture.
7. Carts and other means of transportation.

Appendix 6

Statistical Fragments About the Austrian Empire

Located almost in the middle of Europe and in immediate contact with fourteen different States along an immense perimeter of almost four thousand geographical miles, powerfully influencing for several centuries in the wars and the treaties which changed so many times the aspect of Europe, ruled for several generations by monarchs who were zealous promoters of popular education and of progress in all the sciences, which contributed more than anything else to the welfare of the people and to the strength of the States, the Empire of Austria appeared to be able to offer in its statistics whatever it takes to amply satisfy the wishes of all those who pursue this type of study. Unfortunately for science it has turned out differently. It is true that we count a large number of statistical works on this Empire; but so many errors of the most serious kinds mar the most famous works, and the best ones of them present as yet so many lacunae in those parts which today are considered as essential to the statistics of a country that we can affirm without hesitation that the *true statistics* of the Empire of Austria still *remains to be published*. We say *remains to be published* because for a few years now within the offices one is being prepared with the greatest details.

The idea of having a very detailed general statistics prepared is due to two ministers, who in these last years shared the entire confidence of the deceased Emperor, and who, today, are heading the affairs [of the State], because one could not thusly qualify the partial statistical essays, more or less detailed, more or less complete, executed heretofore on a few provinces. These two very enlightened statesmen* have profoundly felt the necessity to establish general statistics for the whole Empire and particular statistics for each of its provinces, in order to have the exact measure of the resources of the Monarchy and a certain

*See the note on page 54, and page 3 of the Introduction.

basis on which to formulate all of the most difficult administrative operations. It is in agreement with their wishes that Emperor Francis I. ordered its execution in 1828, and since then it has been drafted yearly with great precision and with a very judicious choice of all the main data of which the totality constitutes the physical, moral and political statistics of a large empire. All these facts, despite their prodigious numbers and their very different natures, are classified with admirable order and with great lucidity in a sequence of tables drafted under the orders and direction of Baron de Metzburg, Vice-President of the Directorate General of Accounts (General-Rechnungs-Directorium). The high protection, with which the first authors of the statistics honor us and which we can also thank for our present situation so favorable to the pursuit of our scientific works, has gained for us the inestimable advantage of examining it in detail, and we do not hesitate to proclaim it as one of the best drafted and the most complete one of which we have knowledge despite the countless difficulties that M. de Metzburg had to overcome and under whose immediate direction a small number of employees are executing it. Indeed, the various laws which rule the diverse parts of the Empire of Austria lent themselves with difficulty to the regularity of the information sheets sent by the statistical bureau to the various employees of the provinces: exact answers and perfectly comparable data could not be obtained. At present authorized to publish in our *Annuaire Géographique* everything that concerns the population of the Empire in its greatest detail and in its fluctuations, we shall compare with those corresponding details of the largest states of the world. We hope to obtain thereafter the permission to publish the other parts of the statistics. It will be at that time that we shall be happy to fill the gap that the Austrian Empire offers as yet in a science, which, in our days, has seen so many other countries, formerly almost entirely unknown yet in that respect, to come to occupy one of the most distinguished places.

But before offering a few fragments of the statistics of the Empire, relative to the population and to its distribution in its various parts, we believe it necessary to call the attention of the reader on the erroneous judgments held for several years about the number of its inhabitants.

The most distinguished statisticians and geographers of Germany, even those of the Empire of Austria, evaluated not too long ago its population in a very different way. Bertuch, in 1816, estimated it only at 27,715,500 souls. Baron de Liechtenstein in his statistics of this Empire at first gave it only 27,613,000 without the soldiers, and later 28,201,882 by including the latter. Stein, at the same time reduced it to 27,644,015; Hassel to 27,850,000, while Blumenbach raised it to

28,178,836. In 1819, in the second edition of our *Compendio di Geografia*, we have analyzed the causes of these differences. In refuting the estimates of Baron de Liechtenstein as too low, we have demonstrated that the population of the Empire, in that same year, should at least be 29,000,000. The studies of Baron de Metzburg have proved how well-founded was our reasoning and the precision of the facts we alleged, because in the beginning of 1819 the population stood already at 30,106,737, even if the active servicemen were not included.

Despite the positive facts and the reasoning which we have published in that work, in the *Statistique du Portugal* and in different journals, they still persisted in Germany, in France and in England until 1828 to grant only 28 to 29 million inhabitants to the Austrian Empire. We were not a little surprised when we read in one of the first volumes of a very esteemed geographical dictionary, published in Paris in 1824, that this Empire counted only 26,654,560 inhabitants! But our astonishment was quite larger yet when, back in Italy, we took cognizance of a statistical table of that monarchy, published in Vicenza in 1831, in which its population was still only held at 29,499,500 souls, then, when, as we shall see below, at the end of that same year, it had risen to 34,121,668, and that number did not include the servicemen on active duty!

We have drafted the following table to show the reader how vague the data are that were published about the population of the Empire. We have restricted ourselves, with a few exceptions close at hand, to the works published in England, in Germany and in the Empire of Austria, not during the last twenty years, but only during the first months of this year and the four preceding ones. We have added the estimates published by a few journals and by a few justifiably famous almanacs as well as the one given by a distinguished statistician, M. Schnitzler, in the *Encyclopédie des Gens du Monde*. We have not cited the opinion emitted by M. Worcester in the *American Almanac* nor the one of M. Quetelet in the *Annuaire de l'Observatoire de Bruxelles* for the same year and the following one because these two statisticians, conscientious and deservably famous, have preferred to reproduce in their calendars the statistical tables of the *Abrégé de Géographie* — despite the somewhat remote times to which these data referred — rather than run the risk, in more recent tables, of offering to the public elements that cannot be compared and which are for the greater part erroneous. We cannot remain indifferent to such a vote of confidence, flattering as it may be for us, that these two scholars have given us: we feel its impact and we seize this opportunity to address them our thanks.

Comparative Table of the
Principal Opinions Emitted About the Population of the
Empire of Austria in the Works Published from 1831 to 1835

Names of the Authors, Time of the Publication of their Works and Year to which the Population Refers	Number of Inhabitants
Thomas Myers, in his new *Geography*, published in London in 1833, referring to the year 1818 and citing Liechtenstein	28,207,882
Lanzani, in his *Quadro Geografico Statistico della Monarchia Austriaca*, published in Vicenza in 1831.	29,499,500
Vollrath Hoffmann, in *Erde und ihre Bewohner*, published in Stuttgart, in 1834, but without referring to any particular year.	30,006,849
Annegarn, in his *Manuel de Géographie pour la jeunesse*, published in Münster in 1834 — *more than*	30,000,000
The anonymous author of the introduction to the *Géographie pour l'usage des écoles normales et supérieures de l'Empire d'Autriche*, published in Vienna in 1833 and referring to the same year.	30,834,000
Schacht, in his *Géographie ancienne et moderne*, published in Mainz in 1831.	31,000,000
Cannabich, in his *Géographie*, published in Ilmenau in 1832, and referring to the same year.	32,000,000
Schnitzler, in *l'Encyclopédie des Gens du Monde*, and referring to the year 1832.	32,000,000
L'Annuaire Historique Universel of 1834, published by M. Lesur, referring to the year 1833.	32,000,000
Worcester, in his *Elements of Geography*, published in Boston in the United States, in 1832.	32,000,000
The Companion to the Almanac for the year 1833, citing the *Almanac of Gotha*.	32,071,935
Hugh Murray, in his *Encyclopedia of Geography*, published in London in 1834, referring to the year 1829, and citing Colonel de Traux.	32,134,037
Raffelsperger, in his *Reise-Secretär*, published in Vienna in 1834.	32,157,835
Hörschelmann, in the last edition of the *Manuel de Géographie of Stein*, done in Leipzig in 1834, but referring to the year 1831.	32,425,074
Schaden, in his *Tableau Statistique*, published in Munich in 1835, referring to the year 1831.	32,425,074

Names of the Authors, Time of the Publication of their Works and Year to which the Population Refers	*Number of Inhabitants*
The Almanach of Gotha of 1834.	32,500,000
Le Temps, one of the first organs of the French periodical press, in a statistical article on the Empire of Austria, in 1834.	33,000,000
Vollrath Hoffmann, in his *Erde und ihre Bewohner*, published in Stuttgart in 1833 and referring to the year 1831.	33,000,000
Folger, in his *Manuel de Géographie*, published in 1833.	33,000,000
Cannabich, in the *Hausbuch des geographischen Wissens*, published in Vienna in 1834, and referring to the year 1833.	33,281,869
Cannabich, in the new edition of Galletti, made in Vienna in 1835, referring to the same year and including the soldiers.	33,360,000
Norbert Schnabel, in the 7th edition of Galletti, done in Pesth in 1831, and referring to the year 1830. This evaluation was followed by the editor of the Almanach published by the Academy of St. Petersburg for the year 1834.	33,400,000
Blumenbach, in the *Allgemeine Erdkunde de Schutz*, in 1830 and referring to the same year.	33,425,000
L'Almanach Statistique de Weimar of the year 1835, referring to the year 1834.	33,482,692
Malchus, in his *Géographie Militaire de l'Europe*, published in 1832 and 1833 and referring to the end of the year 1830.	33,630,381
Norbert Schnabel, in his *Statistique Générale de l'Europe*, published in Vienna in 1833 and referring to the year 1831.	33,634,700
Bickes, in an article on the productive and military forces of the European States in the year 1833 and published in the *Annales de Weick* in 1834. This evaluation was reproduced by Berghaus in his Annales in 1834.	33,871,173
The *Allgemeine Zeitung* in 1834, referring to the end of the year 1833. This evaluation was reproduced by Berghaus in his Annales in 1834 and by the Almanach de Gotha in 1835.	34,152,348
The *Carte Routière de la Monarchie Autrichienne* published by the General Staff in 1835, and including the	

Names of the Authors, Time of the Publication of their Works and Year to which the Population Refers	*Number of Inhabitants*
soldiers, but without indicating to what year this population should relate.	34,454,681
John MacGregor, in his *Resources and Statistics of Nations*, published in London in 1834 and referring to the same year.	34,500,000
De Traux and Fried, in the new road and postal map, published by Artaria in Vienna in 1833 and dedicated to His Majesty Emperor Francis I.	34,755,400
Horschelmann, in his *Manuel de Géographie*, published in Berlin in 1833, and referring to the end of the year 1831.	35,000,000

In seeing these enormous differences offered by our table, in spite of the short lapse of time it embraces, one cannot refrain from deploring the imperfection into which the first element of the statistics of one of the most powerful states of the world, of an Empire situated nearly in the middle of Europe, has slipped.

What is one to think of all the other statistical documents — official or semi-official — that are being put out above that monarchy, if the first of them all, the one about which the government does not harbor any mysteries, oscillates between numbers which differ between them by one-fifth? Data — even official ones — relative to the population of that empire, which one finds on a few geographical maps, which a few journals give or that one finds in one or the other esteemed work, although *absolutely* exact, cease to have this exactness *relatively speaking* at the time to which they have to be referred. It is in this category that these evaluations must be classified, which, without any indication as to the year they refer, have been published in the ordinance maps, in the one of M. Artaria and others. Induced into error by a so-called official census, which, according to M. Cannabich, was supposed to have taken place at the end of the year 1825 over the whole of the Austrian Empire, and which this scholar has published in the *Ephémérides Géographiques de Weimar* — census which carried the total population of the Empire at 31,624,888 souls — we have thought it possible, without any inconvenience, to estimate it at 32,000,000 for the end of the following year, the time which we had chosen for the editing of the *Balance Politique du Globe*, and to which all the statistical elements had to be reduced for inclusion in its table. However, we were wrong and we shall see below that at that same time it was supposed to have been carried at 33,500,000, soldiers included; that is a million and a half more than our own estimates and several millions beyond the erroneous estimates of all our predecessors.

It is with the documents contained in the official statistics of the Empire that we have drafted the following table. It demonstrates the considerable increase the population has achieved. The only setback occurred in 1832, a year unfortunately memorable on account of the ravages caused by cholera-morbus. It is in the Appendix of our *Annuaire Géographique* that one will find the comparison between the movement of the population in the Empire and the corresponding evolution observed in France, in Russia, in the Prussian, English and Dutch monarchies, in the United States and in a large number of other nations.

Table Offering the Population of the Empire of Austria and its Annual Evolution from 1818 until 1833

Year	Population in the beginning of each year without soldiers	Yearly Increase
1818	29,813,586	--
1819	30,106,737	293,151
1820	30,504,605	397,868
1821	30,848,458	343,853
1822	31,218,852	370,394
1823	31,582,430	363,578
1824	31,974,753	392,323
1825	32,377,570	402,817
1826	32,828,071	450,501
1827	33,211,770	383,699
1828	33,551,241	339,471
1829	33,789,378	238,137
1830	33,991,547	202,169
1831	34,383,517	392,070
1832	34,121,668	-261,849*
1833	34,217,494	95,836

It is still from the official statistics of the Empire that we borrow the following table; it offers its existing population in the beginning of the year 1833, divided into its fifteen large administrative divisions.

*Reduction as a result of cholera-morbus.

Statistical Table
of the Austrian Empire

Large Administrative Divisions	Superficy in Square Miles (of 60 to the degree)	Population in the Beginning of 1833, without the soldiers	
		Absolute	Relative
Lower Austria	5,755	1,284,888	223
Upper Austria	5,571	833,844	150
Styria	6,524	902,408	138
Carinthia and Carniola	5,922	728,179	123
Littoral States	2,325	435,812	187
Tyrol	8,264	811,426	98
Bohemia	15,240	3,936,584	258
Moravia and Silesia	7,712	2,062,906	267.5
Galicia	25,227	4,217,791	167
Dalmatia	3,814	350,388	92
Lombardy	6,307	2,416,567	383
Venetian Provinces	6,875	2,041,180	297
Hungary	66,914	11,223,587	168
Transylvania	16,093	1,930,259	120
Military Outposts	11,426	1,041,675	91
Totals	193,969	34,217,494	176

In order to avoid any misunderstanding we shall observe that the total population of the Empire in the beginning of the year 1833, inclusive of the soldiers, stood at 34,735,702, and that all the facts accumulated to present authorize the belief that in the beginning of this year (1835) it must have capped the 35,400,000 mark. This figure, compared with the estimates published by German, English and French newspapers, which for that same time granted it only thirty-two to thirty-four million, demonstrates how inaccurate the documents, which are often presented as official, really are and must weaken considerably the authority which one could be led to grant to those populations assigned to other nations.

Now we are going to make a few statistical remarks about the facts offered by the last table. We shall begin with the column of the areas.

The following table presents all of the large administrative divisions arranged according to their area in decreasing order. We have added the *average division*, that is to say, the one we would obtain if we divided all the territory of the empire in 15 provinces of equal area.

Large *Administrative Divisions*	Areas *in Square Miles*
1. Hungary	66,914
2. Galicia	25,227
3. Transylvania	16,093
4. Bohemia	15,240
Average Division	12,933
5. Military Outposts	11,426
6. Tyrol	8,264
7. Moravia and Silesia	7,712
8. Venetian Provinces	6,875
9. Styria	6,524
10. Lombardy	6,307
11. Carinthia and Carniola	5,922
12. Lower Austria	5,755
13. Upper Austria	5,571
14. Dalmatia	3,814
15. Littoral	2,325

By examining the table attentively one sees that while *Hungary* exceeds one-third of the total area of the Empire, the *Littoral* is barely the eighty-third part of it, or, in other terms that *Hungary* is 29 times larger than the *Littoral*. Compared to the *Average Division*, these two extreme divisions of the Austrian Monarchy are, *the first* 5 times larger than it and *the second* 5 times smaller. We also notice that only four administrative divisions exceed the average division, to wit: *Hungary, Galicia, Transylvania* and *Bohemia*; all the others are smaller. The *Military Outposts* are closer to it than any other.

Proceeding now with the comparison of the administrative divisions of the Empire of Austria with the corresponding ones of the other great powers, we find* that the extreme counties of the Kingdom of England are the one of *York*, with an area of 4,432 square miles and the one of *Rutland* with one of 112, while the *average county* has only 842. The largest, therefore, exceeds the smallest 39.6 times, or almost 40 times, which is a proportion stronger yet than the one observed between Hungary and the Littoral.

France even, which among the large countries offers more or less regular administrative divisions, is not exempt from this inconvenience. Indeed, we see that while the area of the *average department* is 1,780 [square] miles, that of the *Gironde* is 2,981 when the one of the

We borrow the elements of these comparisons from the Tableaux statistiques des Monarchies Anglaise et Française et de l'Empire Russe, *which we published in Paris. See its titles in Appendix 8.*

Seine is only 138. The largest department is therefore to the smallest as 21.6, or almost 22 to 1, that is to say that the department of the *Gironde* is almost 22 times larger than the one of the *Seine*.

The territory of the Prussian Monarchy offers in its administrative divisions, or in its 25 governments, less irregularity than any of the other great powers. Indeed, while the *average government* has an area of 3,209 [square] miles, the *maximum* — the one of *Königsberg* — counts only 6,480, and the *minimum* — the one of *Cologne* — has 989, which gives a proportion of 6.6 or about 7; that is to say that the largest of the governments does not even surpass the smallest one 7 times in area.

Even by admitting in the comparisons only those parts of the Russian Empire which are organized in governments, enormous differences are found in the apportionment of its immense area. According to the new divisions the area of the new *government of Ienisseisk* is 728,420 square miles; that of the government of *Estonia* is 5,500; this gives the proportion of 1 to 134.4, that is to say that the largest government exceeds by 134 times the smallest government's area. What would it be if we admitted in these comparisons the 16 provinces or *oblasts*! We would find then that while the new province of *Iakutsk* does not count less than 1,057,060 square miles, the one of *Bialystok* has only 2,180, which gives a proportion of 484.9 or 485 to 1; that is to say that the province of *Iakutsk* is almost 485 times larger than the one of *Bialystok*!

In considering the Administrative Divisions of the Empire of Austria with respect to the absolute population, we find that we can list them in the following order:

Large Administrative Divisions	*Number of Inhabitants*
1. Hungary	11,223,587
2. Galicia	4,217,791
3. Bohemia	3,936,584
4. Lombardy	2,416,567
Average Division	2,211,166
5. Moravia and Silesia	2,062,906
6. Venetian Provinces	2,041,180
7. Transylvania	1,930,259
8. Lower Austria	1,284,883
9. Military Outposts	1,041,675
10. Styria	902,408
11. Upper Austria	833,844
12. Tyrol	811,426
13. Carinthia and Carniola	728,179

Average Division	Number of Inhabitants
14. Littoral	435,812
15. Dalmatia	350,388

On examining this table, we see: (1) that only four administrative divisions exceed the population of the average division; they are: *Hungary, Galicia, Bohemia* and *Lombardy*; (2) that three, to wit: *Moravia* and *Silesia*, the *Venetian Provinces* and *Transylvania* are closest to it; (3) that all the others are smaller than it; (4) that *Hungary* alone possesses almost one-third of the total population of the Empire and *Dalmatia* has barely one-ninety-eighth; (5) that *Hungary* is to *Dalmatia* as 32 is to 1, that is to say that the population of the former is thirty-two times that of the latter.

Let us now see in which fashion the population is distributed in the territory of the other large powers. We regret that, not having as yet concluded the calculations begun to adjust to the beginning of 1833 all the statistical elements admitted into the *Balance politique du Globe* and into the *Abrégé de Géographie*, we can now base our comparisons only on the elements found in the above mentioned tables; they all refer to the year 1826, exception made for the population of England, which refers to the year 1821. There exists, however, no great inconvenience in using them because we are treating here only comparisons between different parts of a same country.

The absolute population of the *average department* in France is 327,000 souls; the most populated, that of the *department of the Seine*, is 1,013,000; the least populated, that of the *department of the Hautes Alpes*, is 125,000; the *maximum* is to the *minimum* as 32.1, or 32, is to 1; that is to say that the absolute population of the *department of the Seine* is 32 times larger than the absolute population of the *department of the Hautes Alpes*; it is absolutely the same proportion we have noted to exist between the absolute population of *Hungary* and that of *Dalmatia*.

The population extremes of the Kingdom of England are those of the *county of York*, which has 1,175,000 souls and of the *county of Rutland*, which has only 18,000, while the *average county* would have 230,000. The first two populations offer a proportion of 65.3, or 65 to 1, that is to say that the population of the *county of York* exceeds 65 times that of the *county of Rutland*; this proportion is more than double the one we have just noted in the Empire of Austria and the French Monarchy.

In the Prussian Monarchy the governments with extremes in

absolute populations are the one of *Breslau* with 925,000 inhabitants and the one of *Stralsund* with 143,000, while the population of the *average government* there is 499,000 strong. The population of the first two offers therefore a proportion of 6.4, or 6, to 1, that is to say that the *government of Breslau*, which is the most populated, does not even count six and one-half times the number of inhabitants possessed by *Stralsund*, which is the least populated.

In the Russian Empire the two governments offering extremes are the one of *Poltava* with 1,878,000 inhabitants and the one of *Ienisseisk* with 185,000; these two figures offer the proportion of 10.1, or 10, to 1, that is to say that the most populated government counts only 10 times more inhabitants than the least populated.

In considering the Administrative Divisions with respect to the relative population, they rank as follows:

Large *Administrative Divisions*	*Inhabitants* *per Square Mile*
1. Lombardy	383
2. Venetian Provinces	297
3. Moravia and Silesia	267.5
4. Bohemia	258
5. Lower Austria	223
6. Littoral	187
Average Division of the Empire	176
7. Hungary	168
8. Galicia	167
9. Upper Austria	150
10. Styria	138
11. Carinthia and Carniola	123
12. Transylvania	120
13. Tyrol	98
14. Dalmatia	92
15. Military Outposts	91

Lombardy which, at page 119, was occupying only the 10th rank for its area, in the First Table, and which, at page 120, we have seen climb to the fourth rank in the Second Table, is here heading all the large administrative divisions of the Empire. Following the *Venetian Provinces*, *Moravia* and *Bohemia* occupy 3rd place and 4th place; then comes *Lower Austria* and finally the *Littoral*. All the other large administrative divisions have a relative population lower than that of the *mean division*. The *Military Outposts*, despite the fertility of their soil and the clemency of their climate, offer the least concentrated population of the whole Monarchy; it is four times inferior to that of Lombardy and twice less that of the Littoral. If the whole *Empire of Austria* were as populous as *Lombardy*, it would count no less than 78 million inhabitants whereas it would only possess 17,654,000 of them if its relative population were equal to that of the *Military Outposts*. We have seen that in the beginning of the year 1833, inclusive of the soldiers on active duty, its population counted 34,735,702. That is exactly double what it would count in the second hypothesis and a little less than half of what it would count in the first one.

We reserve for the Statistical Table of the Earth a host of other comparisons between the Empire of Austria and the principal states of the world. Here we shall restrict ourselves to observe that that empire occupies the 19th rank among all the states of the globe, with respect to its area, and the 4th for its absolute population, because only the *Chinese Empire*, the *British Monarchy* and the *Russian Empire* count a larger number of inhabitants.

For the reasons given at page 121, that is our inability to finish the necessary calculations for the obtaining of comparable elements, we have borrowed from *The World compared with the British Empire** the table below and the two thereafter. However, we have rectified the population and the area of the Empire of Austria in agreement with the official data that we have at hand. The general population refers to the end of the year 1826; we have carried back to 1822 the so-called census of 1825, which has served us in the calculations of the English table.

Comparative Table of the Relative Population of the Most Populous Provinces of the Empire of Austria and of the Principal States of the World

Names of the States and of Provinces	Year	Area in Square Miles	Inhabitants per Square Mile
Empire of Austria	1826	194,000	173
Lombardo-Venetian Kingdom	1822	13,631	311
Milan	--	766	616
Mantua	--	437	554
Cremona	--	362	499
Padua	--	637	467
Vicenza	--	659	454

*But with the improvements we have brought to it in the Italian edition of the *Bilancia Politica del Globo,* which we published in Padua in 1833.

Names of the States and of Provinces	Year	Area in Square Miles	Inhabitants per Square Mile
Polesina	--	331	424
Treviso	--	570	416
Moravia and Silesia	--	7,704	256
Teschen	--	554	320
Prerau	--	872	289
Troppau	--	771	285
Kingdom of Bohemia	--	15,249	243
Bidschow	--	717	338
Königgrätz	--	976	322
Leitmeritz	--	1,096	308
Chrudim	--	941	307
Bunzlau	--	1,235	305
Kingdom of Galicia	--	24,768	173
Wadowice	--	1,046	301
Bochnia	--	790	261
Sandec	--	922	249
Iaslo	--	966	231
Archduchy of Austria	--	11,338	177
Hausruck	--	696	257
Kingdom of Hungary	--	66,900	141
Warasdin	--	547	231
Agram	--	1,728	223
Trentschin	--	1,405	219
Presbourg	--	1,323	204
Russian Empire	1826	5,912,000	10.1
Moscow	--	9,220	145
Kursk	--	12,610	131
Kaluga	--	9,410	125
Podolia	--	11,820	124
Tula	--	8,850	118
Riazan	--	11,310	117
Poltava	--	16,240	115
Bialystok	--	2,180	103
Kingdom of Poland	1825	36,330	106
Mazovie	--	5,540	135
Krakow	--	3,090	131
Kalisz	--	4,750	120
Kingdom of Sweden	1826	127,000	22
Malmahus	1825	1,285	149
Göteborg	--	1,398	105
Blekinge	--	885	97
Christianstad	--	1,777	82
Kingdom of Sardinia	1826	21,000	205
Genoa	--	1,266	477
Alexandria	--	1,474	388
Turin	--	2,086	382
Papal State	--	13,000	199
Ancône	--	485	320
Bologna	--	1,077	284
Macerata and Camerino	--	1,077	227
Kingdom of Portugal	--	29,150	121
Minho	--	2,160	368

Names of the States and of Provinces	Year	Area in Square Miles	Inhabitants per Square Mile
Kingdom of Bavaria	--	22,120	179
Rezat	1822	2,294	231
Kingdom of Saxony	1826	4,341	314
Leipzig	1822	717	341
Kingdom of Hanover	1826	11,125	139
Hildesheim	1825	1,306	251
Kingdom of Württemberg	1826	5,720	266
Neckar	--	1,061	377
Helvetic Confederation	--	11,200	177
Geneva	--	69	761
Appenzell	--	115	457
Zürich	--	517	421
Turgovia	--	203	399
Argovia	--	379	396
Basel	--	139	388
French Monarchy	--	154,000	208
Department of the Seine	--	138	7,321
— of the North	--	1,632	597
— of the Rhône	--	814	513
— of the Lower Rhine	--	1,214	441
— of the Seine-Inférieure	--	1,732	398
— of the Upper Rhine	--	1,120	365
— of the Straits of Dover	--	1,754	348
— of Pas de Calais	--	1,949	331
— of Calvados	--	1,622	308
— of the Somme	--	1,758	298
Isle of *Martinique* in the Antilles	--	270	367
Kingdom of the Netherlands	--	9,780	262
Northern Holland	--	713	568
Southern Holland	--	835	536
Samarang in the isle of Java	1815	869	354
Kadu in the isle of Java	--	614	322
Kingdom of Belgium	1826	8,250	453
Eastern Flanders	--	821	854
Western Flanders	--	920	630
Southern Brabant	--	955	521
Hainaut	--	1,083	511
Prussian Monarchy	--	80,450	155
Düsseldorf	--	1,544	431
Cologne	--	989	379
Aachen	--	1,066	322
Minden	--	1,515	254
Erfurt	--	1,059	253
United Kingdom	--	90,950	257
Kingdom of England	1821	38,200	295
Middlesex	--	212	5,401
Lancaster	--	1,380	763
Surrey	--	571	698
Warwick	--	680	403
Stafford	--	865	394
Kent	--	1,158	370
Gloucester	--	947	355

Names of the States and of Provinces	Year	Area in Square Miles	Inhabitants per Square Mile
Worcester	--	550	336
Hertford	--	398	328
Nottingham	--	630	296
Kingdom of Scotland	--	23,498	89
Edinburgh	--	294	651
Renfrew	--	184	610
Fife	--	355	323
Ayr	--	770	165
Kingdom of Ireland	--	23,000	296
Dublin	--	237	1,160
Armagh	--	314	629
Louth	--	243	511
Down	--	659	494
Monaghan	--	409	427
Longford	--	258	417
Cork	--	1,895	386
Limerick	--	718	386
Bengal, province of British India	--	73,280	345
Dinagepour	--	4,000	743
Bahar, province of British India	--	39,170	281
Bahar	--	3,984	692
Chinese Empire	1826	4,070,000	42
Kiang-Sou	1792	35,200	823
Tse-Kiang	--	29,100	651
Shantung	--	48,400	525
Anglo-American Confederation	1826	1,570,000	7.3
Rhode Island	1830	980	99
Massachusetts	--	6,593	93
Connecticut	--	3,843	47

Appendix 7*

Comparison of Vienna with the Largest Cities of the World, with Respect to the Population

If we want to be of good faith, we must admit that we still do not know exactly the population of the large cities outside of Europe and America. Despite the censuses performed in several regions of Asia and of Australia, and particularly in British India, the greatest uncertainty enshrouds yet everything concerning the number of the inhabitants of Calcutta, of Benares, of Surate and of several other large cities, though the journals and the most esteemed works offer us positive numbers which are exact in appearance.

Shall we, with General Ryd, estimate the population of Calcutta — without its suburbs — between 400,000 and 500,000 inhabitants, or shall we carry it, with the Society of the Schools, to 750,000, for the year 1819, or even to 1,000,000 for the year 1810, with M. Russel, first judge of that city, including all its suburbs? According to the census made in 1822, Calcutta should have only 197,917 inhabitants, because, through some extraordinary circumstance, the whole population of all the suburbs has been excluded. The census of 1798 has given to that city 78,760 houses. Since from that time this number should have increased rather than decreased, it would be absurd to reduce the population of Calcutta below the 500,000 souls mark. M. Hamilton gives it 600,000. We have adopted the estimate of this scholarly geographer. What we have said about Calcutta, we could likewise say about Surate, about Madras, about Benares, Bombay, Delhi and of almost all the large cities of India and of the Isle of Java. We have analyzed the most recent descriptions of the regions lying outside of Europe and we could draft a long table of the singularly differing evaluations given by the geographers and the travelers, almost contemporaries, concerning the population of a same city.

*The lengths of appendixes 6 and 7 have been altered to provide a more logical organization. The separation of Balbi's 6 and 7 would otherwise have come at the Essay...on page 132 instead of here. — Translators' note.

We shall only state that the figures that we offer in this work, without being exact, are, however, those which seem to us to stray the least from the truth. Besides, it is in the chapter *on the population of the cities* of the work that we are going to publish that we invite the reader to resolve his doubts that he might have when he sees us assign to certain cities a population which is very different from the one generally agreed upon but wrongly so. It is good to warn him that almost all the populations of the cities included in the table below refer to the end of the year 1826; only a small number of them must be referred to the following years up to and including 1831.

Names of the Cities	*Number of Inhabitants*
London, capital of the British Monarchy	1,624,000
Peking, capital of the Chinese Empire	1,300,000
Tokyo, capital of the Japanese Empire	1,300,000
Paris, capital of the French Monarchy*	890,000
Hangchow, in the Chinese Empire	600,000
Calcutta, capital of the Anglo-Indian Empire	600,000
Benares, in the Anglo-Indian Empire	600,000
Constantinople, capital of the Ottoman Empire	600,000
Miako, or Kio, in the Japanese Empire	500,000
Canton, in the Chinese Empire	500,000
Nanking, in the Chinese Empire	500,000
Kingtschin, immense village of the Chinese Empire	500,000
Madras, in the Anglo-Indian Empire	462,000
Saint Petersburg, capital of the Russian Empire	449,000
Naples, capital of the Kingdom of the Two Sicilies	364,000
Vienna, capital of the Austrian Empire	330,000
Cairo, capital of Egypt	330,000
Patna, in the Anglo-Indian Empire	312,000
Lucknow, capital of the Kingdom of Aoudh, Anglo-Indian Empire	300,000
Manchester, in England	271,000
Lisbon, capital of the Portuguese Monarchy	260,000
Moscow, in the Russian Empire	250,000
Delhi, in the Anglo-Indian Empire	250,000
Berlin, capital of the Prussian Monarchy	240,000
Dublin, in Ireland, in the British Monarchy	204,000
New York, in the Anglo-American Confederation	203,000
Glasgow, in Scotland, in the British Monarchy	202,000
Amsterdam, in the Dutch Monarchy	201,000
Madrid, capital of the Spanish Monarchy	201,000
Hyderabad, capital of the Kingdom of Dekkan, in Anglo-Indian Empire	200,000
Isfahan, in the Persian Kingdom	200,000
Aleppo, in Syria, in Ottoman Asia	200,000
Mirzapur, in the Anglo-Indian Empire	200,000
Dacca, in the Anglo-Indian Empire	200,000

See what we say in Appendix 4 on the population of this city.

Names of the Cities   *Number of Inhabitants*

Liverpool, in England	185,000
Mexico, capital of the Mexican Confederation	180,000
Palermo, in the Kingdom of the Two Sicilies	173,000
Philadelphia, in the Anglo-American Confederation	168,000
Murshudabad, in the Anglo-Indian Empire	165,000
Lyon, in the French Monarchy*	165,000
Bombay, in the Anglo-Indian Empire	162,000
Edinburgh, in Scotland, in the English Monarchy	162,000
Surate, in the Anglo-Indian Empire	160,000
Rome, capital of the Papal States	154,000
Milan, in the Austrian Empire	151,000
Osaka, in the Japanese Empire	150,000
Nara, in the Japanese Empire	150,000
Cashmire, in the Seikh Confederation	150,000
Birmingham, in the British Monarchy	147,000
Marseilles, in the French Monarchy	145,000
Rio de Janeiro, in the Empire of Brazil	140,000
Warsaw, capital of the Kingdom of Poland, in Russian Empire	140,000
Manila, in the Philippines, in Spanish Pacific	140,000
Damascus, in Syria, in Ottoman Asia	140,000
Tehran, capital of the Kingdom of Persia	130,000
Smyrna, in Anatolia, in Ottoman Asia	130,000
Leeds, in England, in British Monarchy	123,000
Turin, capital of the Sardinian Kingdom in Italy	122,000
Hamburg, in the Germanic Confederation	122,000
Barcelona, in the Spanish Monarchy	120,000
Bahia, in the Empire of Brazil	120,000
Prague, in Bohemia, in the Austrian Empire	120,000
Punah, in the Anglo-Indian Empire	119,000
Nagpur, capital of Kingdom of Nagpur, in Anglo-Indian Empire	115,000
Copenhagen, capital of the Danish Monarchy	115,000
Venice, in the Austrian Empire	114,000
Havana, (Isle of Cuba) in Spanish America	112,000
Bordeaux, in the French Monarchy	109,000
Halifax, in England, in the British Monarchy	109,000
Cork, in Ireland, in the British Monarchy	107,000
Bristol, in England, in the British Monarchy	104,000
Brussels, capital of the Belgian Kingdom	100,000
Baroda, in the Anglo-Indian Empire	100,000
Lahore, capital Kingdom Lahore, in Seikhs Confederation	100,000
Ghandahar, in the Kingdom of Kabul [Afghanistan]	100,000
Herat, capital of the Kingdom of Khorassan [Persia]	100,000
Balfrush, in the Kingdom of Persia	100,000
Tauris, in the Kingdom of Persia	100,000
Ahmadabad, in the Anglo-Indian Empire	100,000
Ugein, in the Kingdom of Sindh	100,000
Huè, in Cochinchina, capital of Empire of Annam	100,000
Saigon, (Kingdom of Cambodia) in Empire of Annam	100,000
Adrianople, in the Ottoman Empire	100,000
Tokat, in Anatolia, in Ottoman Asia	100,000

Inclusive of la Guillotière *and* la Croix-Rousse.

Brussa, in Ottoman Asia	100,000
Baghdad, in Mesopotamia, in Ottoman Asia [Iraq]	100,000
Erzerum, in Armenia, in Ottoman Asia	100,000
Jigagunggar, in Tibet, in Chinese Empire	100,000
Tunis, in the State of Tunisia, in Africa	100,000

Statistical Table
of the Relative Population of the Surroundings of Vienna Compared with the Corresponding Population of the Surroundings of the Largest Capitals and of the Most Populous Cities of Europe and of America

It is useless, or to put it better, absurd, to want to pass judgment on the intensity of the population of two countries of very small area when each one of them has a large and populous city. Indeed, what could one surmise by seeing in the Statistic Table of Europe, published in the *Abrégé*, that the relative population of the republic of Hamburg is 1,302 inhabitants, that the one of the republic of Bremen is 980, while the relative population of France is only 208 and that of the Empire of Austria 165? If one were to describe a circle of 20 to 30 miles around every large city of Europe and around the capitals of all its small states, we would find that the relative population of the areas of which these large cities would occupy the centers not only is equal to that of all these states of little area and to that of the small, most populous islands but also that it is often by far more superior to them. However, it is from that erroneous standpoint that quite a few geographers and famous statisticians even have considered and do consider yet the Isle of Malta as the most populous country in the world, and Iceland as the most lacking in people!

Considering that in our *Tableau Physique, Moral et Politique des cinq parties du Monde* we are going to examine a comparison between the relative populations of the surroundings of London, of Paris, of Saint Petersburg, of Vienna, etc., and those of several other large cities of Europe and of America, we have thought it necessary to surround them with an area that should be proportionate to the number of their inhabitants. According to that principle we have assigned an area of 3,200 square miles to the cities whose population was 300,000 souls and above, 2,000 square miles to those with less than 300,000 inhabitants, and 1,500 to those cities, which, as *Naples*, *Palermo*, etc., being oriented in a semicircle on the coast can only have half of the area which surrounds the cities inland, such as *London, Hamburg* and others. In the surrounding area of *Constantinople* we have included a part of the opposite coast of Asia; in that of *Copenhagen*, a fraction of Sweden; a part of the territory of the grand duchy of Baden has been included in the area surrounding *Strasburg*. Everyone can easily understand the reason for our proceeding that way, especially when we see the county of Middlesex, which, though it contains the most populous city of the world, offers a relative population lower than that of the Department of the Seine. This stems from the fact that the area of the county of Middlesex is almost double that of the department of which Paris is the chief town and these administrative divisions are both too small when compared with their respective capitals to enable us to judge their relative populations.

The following table, drafted from the above cited work, has already been published in the one which has the title of *The World compared with the British Empire* and reproduced in the *Bilancia Politica del Globo*. All these populations have been calculated in the first work for the end of the year 1826. We have felt the need to modify ever so little the population count of the surroundings of Vienna, which, for the reasons set forth above, we had underestimated previously.

Cities	*Area in Square Miles*	*Inhabitants per Square Mile*
Naples	1,500	930?
London	3,200	781
Lille	2,000	612
Brussels	2,000	583
Paris	3,200	540
Amsterdam	2,000	487
Milan	2,000	482
Genoa	1,500	472
Venice, with the Lagoon	1,660	465
Stuttgart	1,700	411
Oporto	1,500	400
Rouen	2,000	396
Turin	2,000	384
Lyon	2,000	383
Constantinople	3,200	350?
Zürich	1,385	346
Florence	2,000	340
Palermo	1,500	335?
Frankfurt on the Main	1,500	320
Strasburg	2,000	318
Vienna	3,200	302
Dresden	2,000	300
Lisbon	1,500	290

Cities	Area in Square Miles	Inhabitants per Square Mile
Prague	2,000	286
Breslau	2,000	255
Moscow	3,200	238
Marseilles	1,500	236
Rome	2,000	227
Berlin	2,000	219
Nantes	2,000	209
Copenhagen	2,000	203
Warsaw	2,000	197
Philadelphia	2,000	195
Mexico City	2,000	192
New York City	1,500	191
Boston	1,500	178
Havana	1,500	154
Saint Petersburg	3,200	150
Munich	2,000	147
Baltimore	2,000	93
Stockholm	2,000	84

Essay of a Statistical Table of the World, preceded by the exposition of the general principles of Comparative Statistics, and followed by a cursory view on the area of the Empire of Austria, on its population and its evolution compared to their correlatives in the principal countries of the World.

The *Discoveries by travelers, the natural phenomena* and the *political transactions of the states,* these are the three principal reasons why a geographer cannot, no matter what meticulousness he may strive for in his bookdraft, and were it only for the span of a small number of years, forever present the present state of the earth. For as little a time as the drafting, or even the printing, of his work may take, his treatise will no longer offer in all its parts the order of things he has undertaken to describe. Publishing additions for each change that occurs would be too fastidious a thing for the reader and for the author both; besides that would be the task of a journal because it is the role of the periodic press to announce the remarkable changes that the earth is subjected to in all its facets. To make a new edition is an impossible task when this applies to as considerable a work as ours. We had thought that we could circumscribe this inconvenience and always keep our *Abrégé* current by publishing a few leaves yearly, which, under the same format, with the same printing characters, and under the title *Annuaire Géographique,* or *Complément de l'Abrégé de Géographie,* would present all the changes which would have taken place during the preceding year for the three reasons we have just identified.

Anyone can feel the necessity for this publication when he thinks that the thirty months which have been spent for the printing of our *Abrégé* have sufficed to require modifications in the text, either concerning the government of several states of the *Germanic* and *Helvetic Confederations* and of the present *Kingdom of Poland,* or in the number of the states such as the *Kingdom of the Netherlands,* which no longer exists and has been replaced by the two independent Kingdoms: the one of *Belgium* and the one of *Holland;* the *Republic of Colombia,* which split up into three confederate states, called *New Grenada, Ecuador* and *Venezuela;* or else yet in the description of the cities, on account of the disasters that several of them suffered, such as *Antwerp, Brussels, Liege, Ghent, Bristol,* etc. If our numerous contacts have enabled us to present the results of the latest explorations in Africa, in America and in the Pacific before they were published, it is nonetheless true that once our book will have been published our only recourse will be the *Annuaire* to list in it the new facts — the benefits of the explorations under preparation and of the travels presently being made.

We intend even to publish in this *Annuaire* the *Tableau Statistique des cinq parties du Monde,* adding to it the names of the sovereigns who govern the different countries, and those of the first presidents of the Confederations or of the Republics. What we have seen accomplished by one man only, when he controlled the destiny of France, by Bolivar in South America, by Radama in Madagascar, by Tamchamcha in the Hawaiian Archipelago; what we are presently witnessing by Mahmoud and Mehemet-Ali in the Ottoman Empire, by Fath-Ali-Shah in Persia and by Randjit-Singh in the northwest of India, demonstrates how important it is to know the sovereign or the president who heads the States. After saying what we stated with respect to the statistical data offered by our tables, it becomes quite clear that we are not going to go to the useless lengths of presenting every year the present, respective state of affairs of each country, an impossible target if one is to offer solely data subject to comparison; however, for each state, we shall bring these same data in harmony with the changes that their borders might have undergone. Our *Annuaire* will also register not only all the changes that could have been brought about in the description of each country by the opening of a new canal or inauguration of a new railroad line, the creation — or suppression — of an important literary establishment, the erection or the demolition of a remarkable building, or the ravages caused by fires, epidemics, earthquakes, volcanic eruptions, crestings of rivers, intrusions of the sea and other causes of a similar nature in the cities; but we shall also insert in it any corrections of our errors, which may have escaped us and which would have been brought to our attention by our numerous collaborators or by all the people who love the progress of geography.

It was thusly that we expressed ourselves in September of 1832 in the Introduction of our *Abrégé de Géographie*, one month before its publication. Back in Italy, we set out to work at our task as soon as our health permitted any activity. Without being held back by praise, with which the periodical press of all the nations and of all the colors had honored our work, we scanned it from one end to the other and found nothing but defects and shortcomings. Not forgetting that our description of Europe had been drafted to conform to three different frameworks, that is to say, first for a work which was to form a volume of from 600 to 700 pages, later a volume of 1,000, finally one of 1,500, we knew that its first parts were not in the least in harmony with those of its middle nor the latter with the first and the last ones. We saw therefore that we had to add, broaden, sometimes even subtract to offer a homogeneous whole in all its parts. As a consequence, we have totally reworked the topography of Switzerland, of the Prussian Monarchy, of the Germanic Confederation, a large part of those of the Empire of Austria, of the Belgian Kingdom and of the present Kingdom of the Netherlands. We have felt the full extent of the reproach of one of our very best friends, M. de Larenaudière, in the eloquent and vivacious article he published in the *Nouvelles Annales des Voyages* about our *Abrégé*, and we have given the topography of France all the consideration that the high ideal with which our work had been drafted required of us.

Other important additions and corrections have been suggested to us by esteemed scholars, who, in a host of newspapers, each one in his own article, have signaled that part, which, in their opinion, seemed weakest. All these additions having thickened an already-too-voluminous book, we have attempted to find a way to make enough deletions so as to preserve the original pagination, without leaving anything out that is essential to the teaching of the science that it must accomplish.

It is necessary to distinguish between two entirely different parts in the *Abrégé*: *Geography* for and by itself, the *Introduction* and the *dissertations* or observations intercalated in the body of the work, forming the chapters which furnish the explanation to the statistical tables of the five parts of the world. The innovative nature of the plan of our work, the still imperfect state of the science it treats and the renown enjoyed already for so many years by geographies made available to everyone, demanded on our part the rational account of our method and of the motives which led us to grant preference to those figures that we offered in our tables, figures that were so often opposed to those that had been adopted by our predecessors. But what was necessary for the first edition — and even for the second printing — no longer holds for the new reprint. More than eight thousand copies disseminated among the public and received with extraordinary favor, eight translations made in the principal languages of Europe,* and all this in the short time of less than three years, demonstrate to what extent our method was considered as a good one and also the preference which the public and the scholars alike have granted for the results of our long and difficult geographical and statistical studies. In that spirit, we thought we could omit without any inconvenience all the parts of the Introduction which treated of statistics as well as the five chapters which precede the statistical tables of Europe, Asia, Africa, America and the Pacific. All these facts, considerably augmented and coordinated in such a way as to give it doctrinal substance, all these facts, deleted from the body of the work, will form the first part of the first *Annuaire Géographique*. It will be some sort of introduction to the series of *Annuaires* which we shall publish to keep our *Abrégé* constantly current.

Following the new plan we had drafted for ourselves, we had already finished all the *Additions à l'Europe*, when we were pleasantly surprised to read in the *Allgemeine Zeitung* the announcement of the *Hausbuch des geographischen Wissens*. Indeed, what better reward could we receive for our long sleepless nights than seeing our *Abrégé* serve as a model and basis for the elite of German geographers in order to build a new geographical monument? We did not have the slightest doubt to find all the errors corrected in it, those that could have escaped us formerly; to find all the lacunae filled, lacunae caused by the lack of documents or of time, which had forced us to let them subsist; finally, intercalated in its different parts and in their appropriate place all the new facts by which science had become enriched during and since the printing of the *Abrégé*. But what a great disillusion as we were perusing the *Hausbuch* and still finding in it not only most of the errors that had escaped us, but even new ones added by our so-called correctors. We found practically none of these new facts that recent explorations or works of scholars had just added to geography; not even the considerable changes that certain countries had undergone in their administration.

It is in this vein for example that at pages 435 and 579 of the

---

*Although the first print was in 4,500 copies, thirteen months later, a second printing was necessary. Three years have not yet elapsed since its publication and already we count two German translations, two Italian ones, one English one, and one in the Czech language or Bohemian; it is now being translated into Modern Greek and Spanish; and they assure us that it will be translated into Russian and Arabic.

Hausbuch we found again the typographical errors *Lickmansworth*, in Bedford County, for *Rickmansworth*, in the table of administrative divisions, and, in those of the Ottoman Empire the city *Mezestéré*? and that at page 432 the English Parliament is still described as it was before the memorable reform it just underwent. At page 321 we read with surprise that "the *Niger* or *Dschioliba* is after the *Nile* the best known river of Africa"! At page 21 we still find the *Itacolumi*, in the Sierra do Espinhaço, offered as the culminating peak of the whole Brazilian system, when the measurements just made by Dr. Sellow now force us to consider as such the Peak of the Sierra da Mantequeira, which exceeds it by almost 400 *toises* [toise=6.395 English feet] in height. At page 211, instead of indicating that the *Tagal* is not identical with the *Djede* but are two different volcanoes in the chain of Java, according to M. Blume, they add several points of mediocre height, in contrast with the intended plan of the *Abrégé*, which gives only the culminating point of each chain. At the following page we have in vain been looking for the culminating point of the chain of Morumbidge, which, not having less than 1,400 toises of elevation must be considered as the highest point of the complete eastern part of the Australian system proper.

After the publication of the first installments of the scholarly work of M. Berghaus on Asia, work which offers the gathering of everything we know as most positive and most recent on that part of the world and on the lands of Oceania, which the German geographers consider as its appurtenances, we expected to find in the *Hausbuch* the Philippines described in the light of the official documents published on that archipelago by the scholarly editor of the *Annalen der Völkerkunde*; but all we found there was the literal translation of what we had recorded in the *Abrégé*.

Similarly, we have not found anything added to the topography of the states of Asia, of Africa, of America and of Oceania despite the host of new facts that have already been gathered. We shall not prolong these critical remarks so that we should not be suspected of harboring views we are far from holding as we are writing them. We beg permission to make only two more remarks. At page 276 they restrict themselves to the translation of the *Abrégé*, which was the first to signal the demise of Velled Sélassié, who, according to rightfully esteemed geographies, newspapers and almanacs, published in 1832 and 1835, still reigns on the Tigré, although this sovereign has been dead for several years; however, accounts already two years old announce the death of Subgadis and name another warlike usurper who has replaced him on the throne of Tigré. Not knowing what Captains Kotzebue and Beechey have published on Easter Island, the translator of our Oceania, apparently bent on correcting our errors, represents* its misshapen colossi as still existing, when in the *Abrégé* we had already indicated that only their ruins can still be seen, in accordance with the reports of these famous navigators!

However, it is only right that each of the authors of the *Hausbuch* be paid his due. Having worked separately we shall now make allowance for each one of them.

We shall first begin by separating from the others the famed author of the *Gea* and the illustrious astronomer who directs the observatory of Vienna. Their scholarly and conscientious work, their delicate method and attitude toward the author of the *Abrégé* demand this separation.

M. *Zeune*, whose geographical works justly commended are raised quite high among the German geographers, has taken up the translation of the *Principes Généraux* and that of the *description of Asia*. Perfectly informed of all the progress made by the geographical and historical sciences, the author of the *Gea* knew how to appreciate all the difficulties we had to overcome in the drafting of these two parts of the *Abrégé*; he recognized the value of our preceding works and of the experience we had acquired through more than 25 years devoted to these studies; he respected the opinions of Ritter, Humboldt, Klaproth, Abel Remusat, Champollion, Larenaudière, Bournouf, Walckenaer, Rainaud, Lesson, Guillemin and other famous scholars, whose works or kind communications we had cited. Foregoing the role of original author, M. Zeune confined himself to the one of faithful translator. However, he took the liberty of intercalating a few remarks into the text, always between parentheses and finished by the initial of his name. In this fashion the reader recognizes always what belongs to us and acquires sometimes some important knowledge or finds useful explanations. Faithful in the carrying out of his translator's task M. Zeune has scrupulously reproduced the whole chapter which serves as introduction to the statistical table of Asia. He did more yet: he made our meteorological table of the world more interesting by adding at the end of the *Principes Généraux* the one of M. Löwenberg, which we can consider as the most complete work ever published on this subject.

M. *Littrow*,† for whom an excellent treatise of *Métrologie* could

---

*Page 291 of the Hausbuch *and page 1283 of the* Abrégé.

†M. Littrow, *famous mathematician and astronomer, formerly professor at Kazan and for a few years professor of astronomy at Vienna and director of the observatory of that university, is one of the most active writers of Germany. Not counting a large number of articles, published in his main newspapers, articles which are as remarkable by their display of erudition as they are by the style, M. Littrow has already published about thirty works, all of them justly praised. In this number are*

have given him the right to revise the *table of the monies*, of the *weights* and of the *ancient and modern measures*, drafted by M. Guerin de Thionville for the *Abrégé*, abstained from changing anything. An intelligent and impartial appreciator of the nice and scholarly work of our friend, M. Littrow confined himself to translating it faithfully. Fully conscious of the objective the editor desired to reach by publishing the *Hausbuch*, he added next to the monies, weights and metric measures, the monies, weights and measures in use in the Empire of Austria. In this fashion he made this part of the *Hausbuch* more complete than that of the original, and incomparably more useful for the Germans and especially for all the inhabitants of the Austrian Empire.

On the same level of the works of MM. Zeune and Littrow we shall gladly list the one made by *M. Sommer* about *America*, which, strictly speaking, is only a literal translation of that part of the *Abrégé*, if this scholar had not taken the liberty of making so many important deletions and if he had not added the populations of the provinces in our tables of the administrative divisions of the states of that part of the world, populations which we had an excellent reason to exclude from our work, and which are a far cry from making it better. The changes which M. Sommer has allowed himself to make in the translation of a large number of articles and in particular in the one concerning the distribution of the inhabitants according to their races,* in the one of the statistics of the United States† and in the article concerning the social status of the Americans,§ articles which we have pulled out from our files as well as the two other ones on the social status of the Africans and the people of Oceania, seem to have been made with the intention of removing the honor of their drafting, a result of long and laborious studies. Not satisfied with deleting almost everything we state at pages 1177-1181 to back up our calculations on the population of America, M. Sommer, through his inconceivable negligence — because we choose not to attribute this to any other motives — reproaches us for giving only 250,000 inhabitants, in 1826, to the Confederation of the Rio de la Plata while M. Müller carries it to 600,000, and this,

(cont.) especially included the Annales de l'Observatoire de Vienne, *which count already 15 volumes in folio; a* traité d'astronomie théorique et pratique *in 3 volumes; another* traité d'astronomie populaire, *in 2 volumes; a* traité de géometrie analytique, *in one volume; the* Calendariographie, *or the science of setting up all types of Calendars, one volume in 8°; a* traité sur les rentes viagères et les pensions des veuves, *in one volume; a* traité de Dioptrique, *serving as introduction to the art of making eyeglasses, likewise in one volume.*
*At page 37 of the Hausbuch and 969 of the Abrégé.
†At page 104 of the Hausbuch and 1041 of the Abrégé.
§At page 61 of the Hausbuch and 990 and 991 of the Abrégé.

when, at page 1179, we are mentioning ourselves the absurdity of the evaluations of Hassel and of other statisticians, who, through an unforgiveable mistake carry it to 2,200,000 souls, and when, in our statistical table of America, at page 1184, we see that we are granting it 700,000 for the same year!

It is with much affliction that we see ourself forced to judge with even more severity the *translation* of *Africa* and of *Oceania* made by M. Wimmer. Without the slightest concern for our copyright, this scholar allows himself to delete or to modify in almost all our general articles of the *Abrégé* all or almost all our citations, even those of our works still in the manuscript stage, by attributing sometimes our work to imaginary authors. Here is an example of this which we take at random. At page 225 of the *Hausbuch*, after having deleted what we said when speaking of the languages of Oceania by referring to our *Atlas Ethnographique du Globe* — which is the first work in which all the peoples of that part of the world have been classified according to the languages they speak — he translates the text of the *Abrégé*, page 1208, which runs: *"Parmi les 78 peuples, dont nous avons classé les idiomes dans l'Atlas Ethnographique du Globe"* etc., by the following: *"Aus den 78 Völkerschaften dieser groszen Familie, welche französische Ethnographen aufzählen etc."* We challenge M. Wimmer to name us just one of these French ethnographers, who, before the publication of the *Atlas Ethnographique* had classified 78 peoples of Oceania according to their languages.

Not satisfied with attacking our literary property by deleting the citations of our own works and by modifying our introductions to the general articles *Etat social des Africains et des Océaniens, Ethnographie, Divisions*, etc., M. Wimmer does not display any greater concern for our numerous collaborators. Thus, in the article *Division et Topographie du Maghreb,** in the introduction† and in the description of the *Biledulgerid* and of the *Sahara*, and in that one§ of the description of the *Nigritie occidentale*, he deletes entirely what we state, announcing the beautiful work of M. de'Avezac, still unedited, that this scholar had put at our disposal and which had been our principal guide in the description of that part of Africa's geography, which is so difficult.

Pressed by the lack of time, not having ourself had the leisure to draft up the extract of that part of the work of Raffles in which the interesting ruins of Borobodo, of Madjaphahit and of Singa-Sari in the

---

**At page 309 of the* Hausbuch *and 877 of the* Abrégé.
†*At page 318 of the* Hausbuch *and 887 of the* Abrégé.
§*At page 329 of the* Hausbuch *and 899 of the* Abrégé.

Isle of Java are described, we gave the knowledgeable résumé which M. Walckenaer made of it in his *Monde Maritime;* this circumstance demanded of us that we cite the source from which we had drawn; M. Wimmer has deleted it entirely. The famous Champollion the Younger, whose irreparable loss is deplored by the historical sciences at the very moment when he was about to let them take one of their most considerable steps forward in a very long time, had had the kindness to offer us his notes and to review himself all our proofs relative to the description of Egypt and of Nubia; and the famous Jomard, who has so much contributed to the development of civilization of modern Egypt, has written its progress with an able hand in the beautiful résumé with which he has gracefully consented to enrich the *Abrégé.* These two circumstances must not have escaped the reader, especially since there is question of subjects foreign to our special studies and which offer doubts on several points, doubts which the scholars are yet far from having dissipated. M. Wimmer, not being stopped by any consideration at all, changes almost entirely* our introduction to the description of Egypt, and refers the reader back to his *Gemälde von Afrika,* published in 1832, for everything that concerns the progress of civilization in that region, which might make one believe that everything that follows is drawn from his own work, when, in reality, it is merely a translation of the *Abrégé.* We encourage the reader to convince himself by comparing the original with the corresponding pages of the *Hausbuch.* The paucity of statistical facts concerning the products of agriculture, which he has added at page 288, had already been furnished to us by M. Jomard; but we had not published them, considering them as foreign to the framework of our work. Similarly, we knew already through an article of the *Ephémérides de Weimar* the new administrative divisions of Egypt, published by Major Prokesch, but we had preferred those given us by M. Jomard for being more complete and for enabling us, with their help, to draft the whole topography of that region, one of the most difficult and most important parts of the *Abrégé.* M. Wimmer's work itself gives credence to what we state because in the translation of the topography of Egypt, instead of following the new divisions he proposes — as he ought to have done — he slavishly follows those we have given in the *Abrégé.* He does more: at page 306, in the table of Arab Tribes, which he adds to our work, and which is far from being an improvement of the *Abrégé,* he classifies them according to the latter [i.e., the *Abrégé's* classification of divisions]!! Relying too much on his own resources, this scholarly geographer, without invoking the slightest imposing authority in his

*At page 285 of the Hausbuch and 853 of the Abrégé.

favor, dares* attack the opinion of M. Braun, the foremost English botanist, with respect to the primitive origin of certain plants, opinion which has been adopted by a famous botanist, by our friend Guillemin, in the article *Végétaux de l'Afrique*, which he had drafted for the *Abrégé*!

But we would never end our task if we wanted to alert the reader about all the changes that an inept hand has inflicted upon the Africa and especially the Oceania of the *Abrégé*. Without the slightest regard for anything we have said in the chapters preceding the statistical tables of these two parts of the world, not only does he delete them but he even formulates reproaches on the number of inhabitants we assign them, a number which is the result of the longest and most difficult research as yet made on that subject, as we shall demonstrate in the work that we are going to publish. But what has struck us the utmost was to see the reproductions of erroneous divisions and denominations — or at least improper ones — of which we had hoped to have purged forever the geography of Oceania. We invite the reader to read in the introduction and in the text of the *Abrégé* what we say when we speak about the *groupe Tasmanien*, of the *archipel de la Pérouse*, of the one of *Quiros*, of the *archipels Mounin-Volcanique et Central*, of those of *Viti*, of *Oua-Horn*, of *Hamoa* or of *Bougainville*, of the *groupe de Kermadec*, of the one of *Toubouai*, of the *archipel de Cook*, of those of *Tahiti* and of *Hawaii*. The experience acquired through twenty-five years of geographical work and the generous cooperation of one of the most scholarly officers of the French fleet, of our friend M. Jules de Blosseville, whom the whole army and science fear not to see again after the first successes he has obtained by exploring the northeast coast of Greenland, were supposed to stop M. Wimmer in the reworking of this part of the *Abrégé*, which is only a literal translation of the text anyway, translation distorted by the displacement of a few of its parts and by the reproduction of unfit names, unknown to the natives and of which several cannot even claim in their favor the advantage of being historical or geographical, not even of being in use since the time of the discovery of the lands upon which they were imposed.

Here we are at *M. Cannabich*, who shouldered the task of translating Europe; we say *of translating* because that is the word that seems applicable to his task, despite the considerable additions he brought to the topography of the *Helvetic* and *Germanic Confederations*, of the *Empire of Austria*, of the *Prussian Monarchy*, despite the prior split of the European part of the *Dutch Monarchy* into the two kingdoms of

---

*At page 253 of the Hausbuch *and* 823 of the Abrégé.*

Belgium and the *Netherlands* and despite the new administrative divisions of the kingdom of *Greece* and the six districts that he has added to the *principality of Serbia*. All the rest of the German geographer's work is only a literal translation of the *Abrégé*, distorted sometimes by the unjustified displacement of several of its parts, by the unforgivable omission of the long chapter which precedes the statistical table of Europe, a long-winded work, a result of all our geographical and statistical studies and to which we do not hesitate to attribute in great part the extraordinary success obtained by our work. We shall see in the *Tableau Statistique de la Terre* what we have to reserve for M. Cannabich regarding the populations he has added to each province and to each city in our tables of the administrative divisions of the States of Europe. However, we cannot refrain from mentioning the inexcusable negligence, offering at pages 71 and following, the populations of the departments of France which the 1832 census assigns them while, in this same table, he allows those which they had in 1826 to stand, a sole exception being the city of Paris; as also giving at pages 435 and following the population of England as it stood in 1821, stating that it was one of the year 1827, and, thereafter, offering for the principality of Wales, for Scotland and for Ireland the populations given them by the 1831 census!

But we must alert the reader to a more singular mistake yet, which we find at page 41. At the end of the article *population*, M. Cannabich makes the remark that the population of Spain exceeds 20 million according to the 1827 census; and so as to eliminate any doubt and that one should not attribute this assertion to a typographical error, he hastens to refer to the table of administrative divisions at page 44, where, indeed, by adding up all the populations assigned to them, we find the sum of 20,000,000. But how do you think this latter figure was arrived at? By adding up the populations of the principal divisions and those of the subdivisions, that is to say by counting twice the number of inhabitants of Old Castillia, of Andalusia, of Valencia and of Murcia!! This singular mistake reminds us of the process used by an Italian geographer which we have identified for the public at page xix. of the Introduction of our *Bilancia Politica del Globo*. This scholar contended he was correcting our evaluation of the area of Asia, which he found to be too small, by adding not only all the areas of the main divisions and of the secondary divisions of India, which we had given in the table published in Paris, under the title of *Balance Politique du Globe*, but by including again the areas of the subdivisions of the latter! We shall mention in this connection an even more singular blunder, which can be found in the pirate edition of the work of our friend Colonel Vacani, made in Florence, and where they summed up the population and the square miles, giving this bizarre end result for the total population of the Hispanic peninsula and of its colonies!!

In summarizing what we have just said about the *Hausbuch*, one can easily see how improper the part of its title is, expressed thusly: *"Frei bearbeitet nach dem Abrégé de Géographie des A. Balbi von Cannabich, Littrow, Sommer, Wimmer und Zeune."* The additions to the topography of a few states of Europe, the interesting meteorological table of M. Löwenberg, the values of the monies, of the weights and of the measures of Austria added to the corresponding metric values in the metrology, the scanty observations intercalated into the text and the transposition of the description of a state, of an archipelago and of a group before or after such or such other state, before or after such and such other archipelago or group, do not give the right to an editor nor to the writers to change the nature of things by transforming simple *Uebersetzer* [translators] into *Bearbeiter* [revisors, reworkers of texts]. The *Hausbuch* is and must only be considered as a *translation* of the *Abrégé*, less the essential parts which have been deleted from it, plus the additions we have just mentioned. As it stands, despite the heterogeneous data that have been inserted, it is nonetheless a book which deserves the favor with which the original has been honored in France, in England, in Italy, in the United States, and in almost all the countries included in the orbit of European civilization.

We know only the first two installments of the *Handbuch der Erdbeschreibung*, which Dr. Charles Andree published in Brunswick from 1834; it is another translation of the *Abrégé*, but even more mutilated and incorrect than the first one. The most heterogeneous data are admitted in it; the most essential parts of our work are excluded from it; we have hardly been able to find any citations in it. For that reason the statistical table of the vegetable and animal kingdoms, which M. Zeune* has faithfully translated with the introduction that precedes it, is to be preferred to the one given by M. Andree† because in the latter's we do not know the authors of the table and, consequently, that work cannot carry any weight, the author of the *Abrégé*, being a statistician, a geographer and a physicist but not enjoying the slightest reputation in the domain of natural history. For that reason we were quite pleased to see the foremost living botanist, the illustrious Décandolle, take the statistical table of the animal kingdom of our *Abrégé* to place opposite to the corresponding table of the vegetable kingdom which he has given, in a remarkable article on the division of the vegetable kingdom in four

---

*Hausbuch *pages lxii and lxiii.*
†Handbuch der Erdbeschreibung *pages 52 and 53.*

large classes, published in volume No. 54 of the *Bibliothèque Universelle*. M. Décandolle for sure would not have honored the *Abrégé*
thusly if he had not found in it the names of the scholarly naturalists
Lesson, Reynaud and Milne Edouards, who by their special knowledge
and by their preceding works could and should give great weight to the
facts they had been so willing to communicate to us to complete
chapter IX. of the *Abrégé*.

Such is the candid, impartial and personality-exempt complaint
we felt we had to lodge against the publication of the *Hausbuch*. We
owed it to our literary rights and to our reputation, which are equally
under attack in it. We have acquired the former and the latter through
the sacrifice of our health and our fortune, and through the sacrifice of
the most beautiful years of our life. It seems that the price is rather high
enough to warrant the right of their preservation. For a long time we
have sought the opportunity of lodging our justified complaints and we
have seized with eagerness the first one that came along. We could not
and we should not have remained indifferent to the blame or the praise
of learned Germany. Indicted in its literary tribunals defenselessly,
because we consider as such defense our *Introduction*, the *five chapters*
which precede the statistical tables of the five parts of the world and the
numerous *citations*, which both science and gratitude demanded of
us, we had to break silence as soon as we were able to do so decently to
enable the public to pronounce themselves in full knowledge of cause
either for the *Hausbuch* or for the *Abrégé*. We hope to have done so
with the moderation, the impartiality and the calmness which must
accompany any literary discussion. Close to 8,000 copies of the *Abrégé*
spread to all points of the civilized world, and the favor with which the
Hausbuch has been received, even make the comparison between these
two books an easy matter everywhere. Let us be judged therefore by
comparing one with the other and we are not doubtful that our
complaints will be found justified. One of the *Hausbuch*'s own collaborators, the famous astronomer, M. Littrow, has already recognized it
in a remarkable article he has published on the *Abrégé* in the
Jahrbücher der Literatur and we learn that other organs of the German
literary press have echoed his voice. If the esteemed editor, M.
Reichard, wanted to give our work to Germany, he should have given
it the way we had made it but not so strangely mutilated as it is found
in the *Hausbuch*. Did he want to make it more palatable for German
use? Then the topographical additions, which we ourselves are
preparing for the third edition and of which a part has already
appeared in the Italian translation, should have been added. But these
additions should have been, like ours, in harmony with the other parts
of the work and not they themselves heterogeneous parts, totally

foreign to the plan and the method followed in the work, as can be noticed in the considerable additions made by M. Cannabich to the topography of the countries we have already mentioned.

Occupied with difficult and exhaustive statistical works as well as by the drafting of works promised long ago to the public, we have neither the leisure nor the desire to interrupt them in order to engage in polemics that our complaint could arouse on the part of some of the collaborators of the *Hausbuch*. We hope that they will be satisfied with the manner in which we have discharged ourselves of this distressing duty. If otherwise, we declare it here solemnly, having appealed before the public, we shall abide by their judgment, and we shall not formulate the slightest response to any retorts which might be addressed us. Let them read our *Abrégé*, let them peruse the works to which it refers, let them thereafter compare it with the corresponding part of the *Hausbuch* and let them judge us with impartiality.

We also seize this occasion to lodge a complaint of another kind against a serious error on the mortality among Russians, which, by a singular mistake one of the most distinguished statisticians attributes to us. In an article *on the proportionate mortality of peoples*, filled with new views and rich in facts and enlightened reasonings, published in 1833 in volume 54 of the *Bibliothèque Universelle*, M. Francis D'Ivernois reproaches us for having stated in the *letter* on the *population of Russia*, which we have addressed to Baron de Férussac, at page 114 of the XVIII.th volume of the *Bulletin des sciences géographiques*, "that the mortality there is lower than in the other countries of Europe. This proportion, in Germany, is 32 to 1. In France it is 30 to 1."

Certain of not having published anything about the mortality of any country, exception made for what we have said in our *Essai Statistique sur le royaume de Portugal*, and in the *Principes Généraux du Traité Elémentaire de Géographie* by Malte-Brun, we cannot conceive how as careful and as scholarly an author as M. D'Ivernois could make us accountable for such a gross error. We have hastened to read the page of the *Bulletin* referred to. Judge of our astonishment when we saw that the esteemed M. D'Ivernois, not having paid any attention to the page where the extract of our letter ends, has mistaken as its continuation the analysis Baron de Férussac makes of the *Tableaux Historiques et Statistiques de l'Empire Russe* by M. Weydemayer. Although the omission of our name at the end of the extract may have contributed greatly to this mistake, the two articles of the *Bulletin* are nonetheless rather distinct by their titles so that they should not be so easily confused. Indeed, the extract of our letter is coded N.76, and the analysis of the work of M. Weydemayer forms article No. 77. Our letter begins at page 104 and finishes at page 109; the analysis made by

Baron de Férussac begins at page 110 and finishes at page 115, and terminates with the initial F.

We are expecting from the loyalty and from the noble character of Sir Francis D'Ivernois, as also from the impartiality of the editors of the *Bibliothèque Universelle* that they do us justice at the first opportunity by indicating their mistake which has brought us such unjust reproaches. The *Bibliothèque Universelle* occupies far too high a position in the periodical literary press that we should see them attribute serious errors to us with indifference — errors we have never committed — and that we should let them confuse us with statisticians whose principles and example we are quite far from professing and from following.

But it is time to come back to the principal subject of this essay. The *Tableau Statistique de la Terre* is composed of three distinct parts, to wit: of an *Introduction*, in which the general principles of comparative statistics are set forth; of the *Political Balance of the Globe*, or of the *General Statistics of the Earth* and of an *Appendix* in which we discuss the area of the Empire of Austria, its *population* and its *evolution* compared with their correlatives in the principal states of the world.

Introduction. The *area*, the *absolute population* and the *relative population*, the *revenues* and the *national debt*, the *land and sea forces* being the main elements of the strength and the resources of a country, they enter also into the orbit of geography and of statistics but with the difference that the geographer is satisfied with general results and that the statistician delves into the more or less large details within each of these elements. So, for example the former is satisfied with knowing that the *area* of the Empire of Austria is 193,969, or 194,000 square miles (of 60 to the degree); the latter, on the other hand, wants to know how many of these 194,000 square miles are destined to the cultivation of cereals or for grazing lands, how many are covered with vineyards, with vegetables, with gardens and with orchards, with special cultivations or else by woods, by waste land, by roads, mountains and rocks; how many of these square miles are covered by built up properties, by ponds, by marshland, by mines and quarries, etc., etc.

The determination of the general statistical results that we have just indicated is quite far from being as easy as the makers of Abrégés of Geography and of Statistical Tables imagine it to be. Their variable nature, which keeps them precise only at a given time, the heterogeneous elements of which some of them are composed, the secret with which all or the greater part of them are enshrouded in certain states, all these demand a mass of preliminary knowledge, a certain experience and a great deal of care to avoid errors and to prevent the admission into one's general work of data that just are not comparable. If professional geographers, if even those who are not professionals, had restricted themselves within these limits and had admitted into their treatises of geography only statistical data drawn from good sources, by identifying them for the reader and indicating the year to which they refer, they would not have muddled everything up and they would not have attracted unjust reproaches for geography and especially for statistics. The limited agreement between the several evaluations of these so-called geographers and statisticians should not be attributed to the imperfection of these two sciences but to the little care of some, to the lack of knowledge, to the presumptuousness or to the bad faith of a large number of others, who, without having made preparatory studies contend to profess one and then the other [i.e., these two sciences]. If in the drafting of a geography or of a general statistics each author were willing to indicate faithfully the source from which he has drawn his figures and the modifications which he has imparted to them, if he indicated at the same time the time to which they must be referred, we would see almost all these so-called contradictions vanish as they are only the necessary and inevitable consequence of the variable elements on which we work.

What we have just said demonstrates the necessity of summarizing everything that concerns the statistical elements which are common to geography and to statistics proper, of coordinating them scientifically so as to offer in their whole the bases on which to construct the calculations that are to be admitted in the statistical table of the globe. That is what we have done in several of the chapters which compose the *Introduction*. We are going to indicate the subject of each one of them.

The I.st chapter offers the large divisions of the globe by determining their areas and their absolute and relative populations.

The II.nd one treats the absolute population of Europe; in the III.rd, the IV.th, the V.th and the VI.th we discuss the absolute populations of Asia, of Africa, of America and of Oceania.

In the VII.th we treat of the populations of the cities by analyzing the chief causes to which we should attribute the astonishing disparity of opinions emitted about the number of inhabitants of one and the same city.

In the VIII.th we speak of the relative population.

In the IX.th we treat of revenues; and in the X.th of the public debt.

In the XI.th we examine everything that should influence the formation of the ground forces; and in the XII.th everything that concerns naval power.

The XIII.th treats of the states. The difficulties encountered by their selection for consideration of the drafting of a general statistics of the globe as well as the determination of the limitations of certain others are discussed. We discuss their titles and the different categories into which we can list them either according to their political importance or according to their titles or else, finally, according to the form of government which rules them. The chapter ends with three tables in which all the states of Europe and of America are classified according to these three very dissimilar ways of considering them.

Political balance of the globe or statistical table of the earth in 1836. This part is the reproduction of the table which we published in Paris in 1828 under the title of *Balance Politique du Globe*. However, all the calculations, instead of referring to the year 1826 as in that one, will refer to the beginning of the year 1833. We have also brought great modifications to this work either by the addition of a few articles or by the modification of certain others. By offering it to the public we are only fulfilling the promise we had made. Occupations of another kind, the troubles that have shaken Europe since its publication and the delay of some documents we were waiting for have obliged us to put off its publication until 1836. This new work, compared to the *Balance Politique* of 1828, could be considered as the greatest proof of the necessity which befalls us to renew entirely every five or six years everything that concerns the statistical part of geography, so great are the changes offered by our new *Balance Politique du Globe* as opposed to the preceding one.

Here are the articles of which the statistics of each state are composed: *Area, absolute* and *relative population, ethnography,* or indication of the different nations which compose the population, *religions,* or indication of the diverse cults professed by its inhabitants, *government, reigning sovereign* or *chief of the state,* by indicating the time of his inauguration, the dynasty to which he belongs, the religion which he professes, etc., *revenue* in francs, *national debt* in francs, *army, fleet, capital city, principal cities, possessions and colonies* for those states which possess countries separated from the principal mass of their territory.

The appendix is composed of three chapters. In the I.st we speak of the difficulties encountered by the drafting of the statistics of the Empire of Austria; in the II.nd we treat of its area; in the III.rd of its population and its evolution as compared with their correlatives in the principal states of the world. These last two chapters are entirely worked out on official documents whose whole is entirely new and of which only a few fragments have been published at different times. It is in this work that we shall analyze everything that has been done by our predecessors on the important subject of the population and its movement in the principal states of the globe. By rendering justice to the conscientious works of *Villermé, Quetelet, Benoiston de Chateauneuf, Humboldt, Malchus, Balbo, Francis D'Ivernois* and of other famous statisticians, we shall have the opportunity of signaling the singular mistakes of several others, who, without being prepared through special studies, not satisfied with engaging in such difficult subjects, have had the ridiculous pretention to outperform professional geographers and statisticians, not hesitating to offer as improvements to that science manifest blunders and mistakes, which they have the gall of proposing in replacement of truths or certain, rather precise limited numbers obtained through long research, which in their lack of knowledge they qualify as errors and of which they present to purge geography and statistics.

This work, which will form a volume in 8° from 450 to 500 pages, will be published in French by M. Jules Renouard, with the same paper and the same characters used in the printing of the *Abrégé de Géographie*, of which it forms the necessary complement. As already stated, it will begin the series of the *Annuaires Géographiques* which must follow the diverse editions of this work. The Appendix will have a different pagination, so that it can be sold separately and to enable the possessors of the *Abrégé* to acquire only that which they will believe to be an essential part of the treatise of geography.

M. Reichard, the editor of the *Hausbuch des geographischen Wissens* has made arrangements with us for the publication of the German translation of our *Tableau Statistique du Globe*. Learned Germany will thusly obtain the necessary complement to the *Hausbuch* and will be able to judge us with knowledge of reason. We have made arrangements so that an Italian translation and another in English will be made simultaneously.

Appendix 8

Chronological List of the Works Published by Adriano Balbi

It is not to satisfy the fancies of a puerile ambition that we are going to offer our readers the list of the works we have published; it is merely to take note of them and to record, so to speak, in the annals of science the precise dates of their publication. Although we have been very pleased with the benevolence with which the periodical press of all the nations and of all the colors has reviewed them, and with the delicate loyalty with which first-ranked scholars and a host of others have cited them every time they have had the opportunity to draw some facts from them, we have, however, had the anguish of watching quite a few other writers, of the rather unscrupulous type, not only pretend not to know of their existence but also claim for their own the fruits of our long vigils and the results of special studies of several scholars or of a few rightly famous statesmen, who were willing to honor us with their publication, for the first time, in our works.

It is in the *Prospetto Politico del Globo* that, already in 1808, we have published, as first author,* a true geography based on basins; it is in the *Compendio di Geografia*, in our thesis on the *Population of America*, published in 1828 in the *Revue Encyclopedique* and in our *Essay on the population of the Globe*, published in the *Revue des Deux-Mondes*, in 1830, that we were first to have attempted to evaluate, with the help of all the most positive facts gathered until then, the approximate number of the inhabitants of the five parts of the world; it is still in this same *Compendio* and in the *Statistical Essay on the Kingdom of Portugal* that, before anyone else, we have alerted the public and the scholars to the extraordinary development that the

---

It is the extract of the Hydrographic, Statistical and Political Atlas of the Globe *still in manuscript stage; it has preceded by a few years all the* géographies by basins *that have been published. Indeed, the one of Hahnzog appeared in Stuttgart in 1812; the one of Major O'Etzel, in Berlin in 1817; and later yet those of M. Charles Hoffmann in Breslau, of M. Denaix, in Paris, etc.*

populations of Europe and of America were experiencing since the
XVIII.th century; it is in the *Ethnographic Atlas of the Globe* that, after
five years of long research, both arid and difficult, and aided by the
lights of the generous cooperation of a large number of scholars and of
travelers, we were able first* to classify all the known, ancient and
modern peoples according to their languages in a scientific and rea-
soned manner, very different from the method followed in the
Mithridates; it is in *la Revue Britannique* in 1831 and 1832 and in the
Abrégé de Géographie, that, by coordinating everything that had been
published heretofore by my predecessors, we have attempted to
identify the principal indigenous and foreign centers of civilization of
Africa, of America and of Oceania; it is finally in the *Statistical Essay
on the Kingdom of Portugal*, in the *Monarchie Française* and in the
Statistical Tables which have followed it that we have tried, also first,
to apply statistics† to the ethics of peoples. The imposition of new
names, a few insignificant changes in the development of the facts, a
few ornaments of style do not suffice to change the nature of things and
transform an *unadmitted plagiarist* into an *original author*. In
publishing the chronological table of our works we believe we are
serving science and guaranteeing simultaneously our literary property
and that of numerous collaborators, who have generously put the
precious documents they had gathered, either in their travels or in their
studies, at our disposal. The public and the scholars will see in it the
precise date of the publication of a *certain order of facts*, that some
more shrewd and ambitious than scholarly and delicate authors do not
blush to set forth as the result of new research or of their own observations.

Year	Title of the Works and Their Price
1808.	*Prospetto Politico Geografico dello Stato Attuale del Globo*, Venice, one volume in 4°. 1 franc 50 centimes. It is the first treatise of elementary geography drafted in ac- cordance with the system of basins.
1817.	*Compendio di Geografia Universale, conforme alle ultime politiche transazioni a piu recenti scoperte; corredato di cinque tavole sistematiche delle principali lingue e di altret-*

---

*See the article published by Malte-Brun in the Journal des Débats (1. December
1826) and volume III of the Mélanges scientifiques et littéraires de Malte-Brun published by M. Nachet, where at pages 413-421 this article has been reproduced.
†See the article published by Malte-Brun in the Journal des Débats (21. July 1823)
when reviewing the Statistical Essay on the Kingdom of Portugal and of Algarva, etc.

Year   *Title of the Works and Their Price*

tante dissertazioni sulla populazione delle cinque parti del mondo. Venice, one volume in 8°.   2 francs.
Elementi di Geografia ad uso de giovanette.
Venice, one volume in 12°.   50 centimes.
It is the abridgement of the preceding work.

1818.   *Prospetto Fisico Politico dello stato attuale del Globo.*
Venice, one table in plano.   2 francs.

1819.   Second edition of the *Compendio di Geografia Universale,* with many additions.
Second edition of the *Elementi di Geografia.*
Many reprints of these two works have been made in Italy but without the cooperation of the author.

1820.   *Tableau Politico-Statistique de l'Europe en 1820.*
Lisbon, one table in plano.   5 francs.

1822.   *Variétés Politico-Statistiques sur la Monarchie Portugaise.*
Paris, 1 volume in 8°.   4 francs 50 centimes
Essai Statistique sur la Royaume de Portugal et d'Algarve, comparé aux autres Etats de l'Europe, et suivi d'un coup-d'oil sur l'état actuel des sciences, des lettres, et des beaux-arts parmi les Portugais des deux hemispheres.
Paris, two thick volumes in 8°.   16 francs.

1826.   *Atlas Ethnographique du Globe, ou Classification des peuples anciens et modernes d'après leurs langues.*
Paris, one volume in folio and one volume in 8°   30 francs.
This work is to be followed by another volume in folio and a volume in 8° under the title *Tableau Physique, Moral et Politique des cinq Parties du Monde.*

1827.   *Essai Historique et Statistique sur le Royaume de Perse.*
Paris, one table in plano, with the map of Persia by Brue.
                                               3 francs 30 centimes.

1828.   *Balance Politique du Globe, à l'usage des hommes d'etat, des administrateurs, de la jeunesse et des gens du monde.*
Paris, one table in plano.   6 francs.
This table has been translated in English in Edinburgh and reproduced almost in its entirety in English and Anglo-American periodical works, in Spanish in Madrid, in Russian in Saint Petersburg, in German in Stuttgart, in Italian in Milan, in Venice and in Bologna.
La Monarchie Française comparée aux Principaux Etats du Monde.
Paris, one table in plano.   6 francs.

Year | Title of the Works and Their Price

1829. *Statistique Comparée des Crimes et de l'Instruction en France,* published with M. Guerry.
Paris, one table in plano. 3 francs.
L'Empire Russe Comparé aux Principaux Etats du Monde.
Paris, one table in plano. 6 francs.

1830. *The World compared with the British Empire.*
Paris, one table in plano. 6 francs.
Le Monde comparé avec l'Empire Britannique.
Paris, one table in plano. 6 francs.

1831. *Essai Historique, Geographique et Statistique sur le Royaume des Pays-Bas.*
Paris, one table in plano. 6 francs.
The historical part is drafted by M. De la Roquette.

1832. *Abrégé de Géographie, rédigé sur un nouveau plan, d'après les derniers traités de paix et les découvertes les plus récentes, etc.*
Paris, 1 volume in 8°. of 1,500 pages. 15 francs.

1833. *Bilancia Politica del Globo, ossia Quadro Statistico della Terra conforme alle ultime politiche transazioni e piu recenti scoperte, seguito da un saggio sulla statistica dell' impero d'Austria.*
Padua, 1 vol. in 8°. of 400 pages. 5 francs.

1834. Second printing of the *Abrégé de Géographie,* with important rectifications and with the alphabetical table of all the proper nouns. 15 francs.

Index